Texture and Color in Needlepoint

Texture and Color in Needlepoint

MICHELE WEAL

HARPER & ROW, PUBLISHERS

New York, Evanston, San Francisco, London

FIRST EDITION

Design by Lydia Link
Photographs by Sanford Rackow; Everett Studios, Inc.
Drawings by Bill Meyerriecks

Library of Congress Cataloging in Publication Data

Weal, Michele.
   Texture and color in needlepoint.
   Bibliography: p.
   Includes index.
   1. Canvas embroidery.   I. Title.
TT778.C3W4   1975   746.4′4   74-1871
ISBN 0-06-014522-6

---

75 76 77 78 79 10 9 8 7 6 5 4 3 2 1

To Bert and David

Contents

Color Plates

Black and White Photographs

Acknowledgments

I extend my grateful thanks to:

All my clients and particularly those who executed designs shown in this book—Elaine Herman Fenton, Wells Fargo Man's Belt; Wendy Furth, Herringbone and Cross Stitch Eyeglass Case; Joyce Gutfreund, Staircase Stripes, and Lady's and Man's Tennis Racquet Covers; Barbara and Sara Hochberg, Spectrum I, Color Version 2; Judith Kaye, Night Garden Headboard, Stars and Stripes Belt, and Afterglow Pillow; Ann Paley, Pillow: Patchwork I, Variation 2; Elaine Rothenberg, Night Sky Belt; Dina Sharack, Staircase and Lattice Work, Color Version 2; Dorothy Spirer, Jacob's Ladder, Lattice Work, Color Version 1, Robbing Peter to Pay Paul, and Mysterious Islands; Deedy Tohn, Lattice Work, Variation 2; Helen Weil, Wall Hanging for Lawyer's Office, and Maureen Winter, Robin's Sampler.

Special people who encouraged and helped me from the beginning:

Wendy Furth, Eleanor Goodman, Audrey Howell, Judith Kaye, Anita Levy, Wilfred Douglas Machin, Jane Nusbaum, Margot Rosenmund, Ruth and Alan Rosenthal, Elaine Stein, and Mary Terry.

Peggy Mitchell, my parents, sister, and brother, whose loving support guided me through my childhood.

Plate 1. Adam and Eve Stool.

Introduction

This book can be used in three ways.

1. You can have the fun of executing the designs by following the step-by-step directions—using my colors or yours. At the same time, you can increase your enjoyment of doing my designs by understanding how they were thought out.

2. You can learn about the integration of stitches: how to do them, use them, and combine them effectively.

3. You can move on to being your own textured needlepoint designer, a theme which runs through the entire book. This book can be a bridge between doing my designs and creating your own. You will, in effect, be obtaining a comprehensive course in intermediate and advanced needlepoint design.

The Mini-Course in Color Fundamentals will help you create your own color compositions. As you work with the stitches and see what effects they create, you will be able to put them into patterns that coordinate the color and texture use.

Through the medium of needlepoint you can experiment and think freely about texture and color. Such personal esthetic development is one of the purposes of art and possibly why so many individuals are turning to needlepoint as an art form. No one is altogether free from convention, but in your needlepoint designing you can be as imaginative as you like.

I suggest you read through the book once, a section at a time, to get the gist of the ideas and techniques offered. Then as you decide what design you want to do or what concepts interest you, go back and read that part more carefully. For instance, before you make your own color version of a design, you would probably want to consult the section on color.

Along with the step-by-step directions for designs, alternative color and texture possibilities are offered in the For Your Own Portfolio sections. You can use the asterisked or starred stitch illustrations as starting points for your own designs. Practical suggestions and advice to help you create your own designs are included in these sections.

Needlepoint is a serious and beautiful subject, and this is the way that I have tried to treat it. That you are reading this book—just the fact that you are a human being with an obvious love for stitchery and needlepoint, a love for art, a love for color—is evidence enough that you can use needlepoint as an artistic and expressive medium.

Texture Through Shading and Stitchery

Needlepoint is a textile art that lies between the extremes of weaving and embroidery. In needlepoint, stitches are worked into an open and firm woven canvas, with the purpose of creating a fabric. The stitches go around, over, and under the canvas threads, reinforcing them and forming one unit, the finished material. The needleworker builds a textile structure in needlepoint and creates a textile surface with stitchery.

As soon as you think of needlepoint as three-dimensional fabric created by stitches, you will start to think of texture in needlepoint. Keep in mind that texture can refer to the illusion of texture as well as to an actual formed texture.

The needlepoint artist can create a feeling of texture as he achieves an illusion of sculptural form. This is a parallel to what many of the great Renaissance

Plate 2. Detail of Adam and Eve Stool.

painters did, and the method has been called chiaroscuro—light–dark shading. In the Adam and Eve stool, chiaroscuro shading is used in the figures of Adam and Eve to suggest the depth of rounded surfaces turning away from you (Color Plates 1 and 2).

A needlepoint artist uses stitches and various types of wools and threads to create a highly varied dimensional surface. This approach is similar to impasto in painting, where the artist uses paint to build up a thick surface. Bumpy, smooth, indented, creviced, and raised surfaces similar to relief sculpture can be created with stitchery. The Cat Pillow (Color Plates 26 and 27), in which shading and stitchery are combined, is an example of this approach. In the unshaded parts, the textures and dimensionality that you feel are real, not illusory. Here, wools, threads, and stitches are used like colored clay.

The medium of needlepoint has been much used for the reproduction of paintings, fabrics, carpets, wallpaper—to paint a picture. But art can involve more than picture-making, more than shading, and more than the creation of the illusion of depth. Twentieth-century art has been experimental and has welcomed the use of real touch-and-feel textures. I believe needlepoint should reflect this. There can be a touch-and-feel needlepoint—not just needlepoint to see.

Notes Applicable to All Step-by-Step Directions

1. Read through the entire directions for each design before buying materials and before starting work. Be sure to read all the information about the design before working from the step-by-step directions.

2. The dimensions for each design are given in inches and, directly underneath, in canvas threads.

▪ Add 6 inches to each of the dimensions given in inches to create a 3-inch margin all around the design. The first dimension given indicates the *height* of the design. The height of the design should be kept parallel to the selvage.

▪ Measure the 3-inch margin on your canvas so that you know where you should start the indication of the dimensions of the design. Now mark off the dimensions using the canvas-thread count. Use a light-gray permanent marking pen or permanent paint to indicate the dimensions of the design.

▪ If your canvas-thread count does not turn out to be exactly the same as the dimensions that have been given in inches, do not be alarmed. There can be a fluctuation from canvas to canvas of the same size mesh in the number of inches and fractional inches a given number of canvas threads will occupy.

3. Bind the raw edges of the canvas. For all my designs I use wide bias tape which I stitch on by machine.

4. If you are unfamiliar with a stitch used in a design, be sure to read the detailed explanation for that stitch and the related information contained in How to Do the Stitches and How They Can Be Combined. Practice any stitches that are new to you in the 3-inch margin of your design.

5. I use Colbert 6* Persian yarn and French canvas. Therefore the ply indicated and the amounts needed will work if you use those same materials. If you use Paternayan Persian yarn and German canvas or other types of materials, be sure to test the ply needed for each stitch on practice canvas to determine what ply yarn and what mesh canvas work best. There may also be a variation in the amount of each color needed.

6. The amount of yarn needed for each design cannot be given in exact terms because each needleworker has an individual way of handling yarn and doing stitches. I have preferred to err in calculating more wool rather than less. You can always use the leftovers for practice pieces and other projects.

7. When working from the color plates and any of the other illustrations, you may find it helpful to set the open book up in a transparent plastic cookbook holder, leaving both your hands free.

8. You can follow my colors exactly. The color numbers for two brands of Persian yarn are provided. However, if you cannot obtain the exact color I used, you will be able to find perfectly adequate substitutes. And more importantly, since this book emphasizes designing your own textured needlepoint, do not be inhibited about making color or stitch changes in my designs that you feel are necessary for your particular situation.

9. When working the designs, keep the selvage of the canvas to your left or right.

10. The use of two colors in some of the Figures does *not* indicate two different color wools. It is meant to make it easier for you, in some cases, to visualize the structure of the stitch, and, in other cases, to visualize one stitch unit at a time.

11. Starred figures can be used as starting points for your own designs.

*If Colbert 6 or Paternayan yarns are not available, use a good-quality Persian-type yarn in the colors you like. See pages 162 ff. for some yarn sources.

ONE

Portfolio of Designs

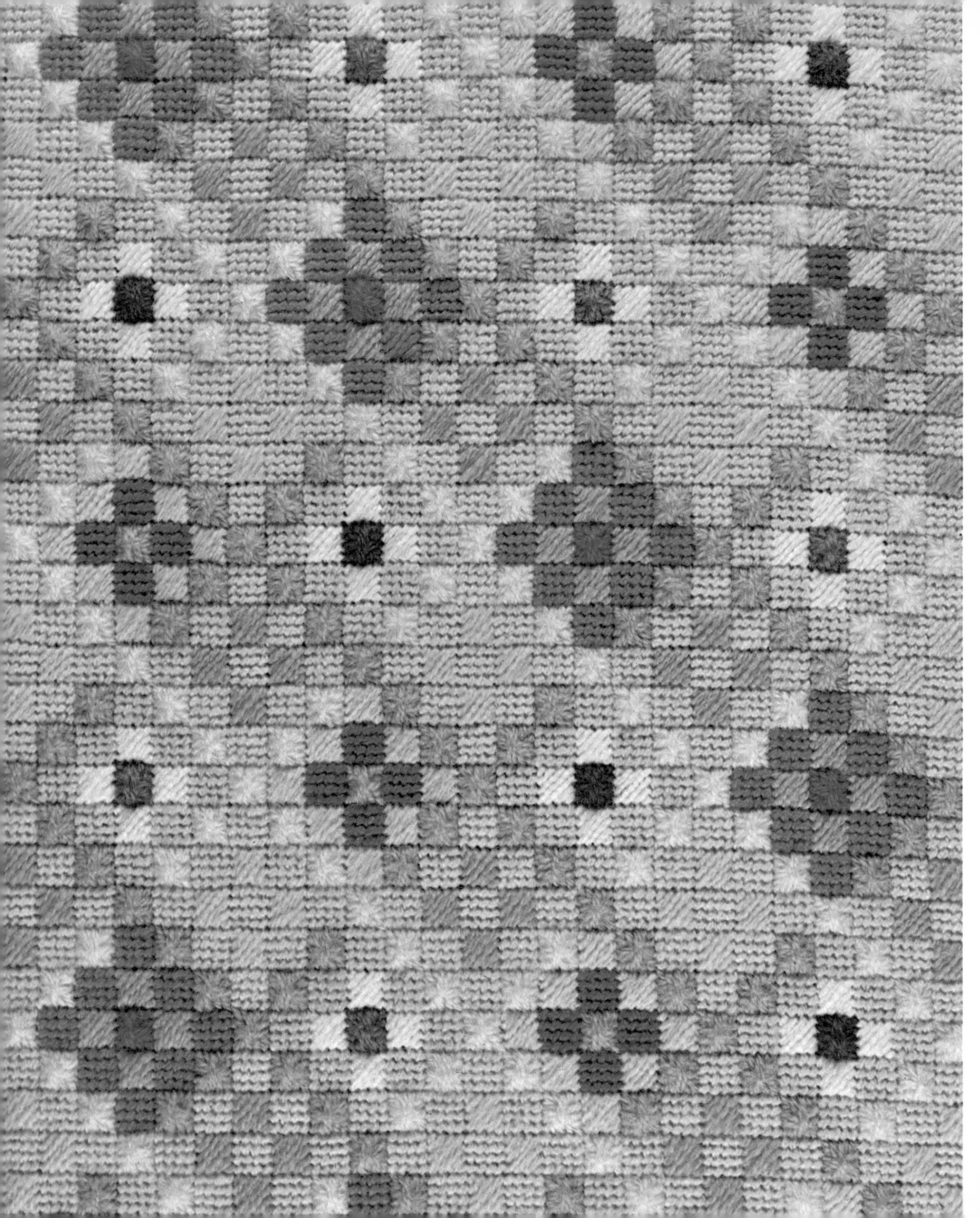

Patchwork I

VARIATION 1

Step-by-Step Directions
[*Color Plates 3 and 4*]

MATERIALS:

No. 12 mono canvas
Persian yarn

DIMENSIONS:

12¼ x 10 inches
140 canvas threads by 108 canvas threads (includes 4 threads for seam allowance all around design)

STITCHES	ILLUSTRATIONS
Tent Stitch	Figs. 5a, 5b, 5c, 5d, 5e
Double Leviathan Stitch	Figs. 4a, 4b, 4c, 4d, 4e
Scotch Stitch over 4 canvas threads	Figs. 8a, 8b

Work from Color Plate **3** to follow the stitch pattern and color scheme. Figs. 1*, 2*, and 2a* show the three stitch patterns used in this design.

Step 1

Set up the framework of the design by counting out and stitching the armatures of the Double Leviathan Stitches that are connected to one another. Use 2-ply yarn.

■ As explained on page 8, the armature of the Double Leviathan Stitch is the basic Cross Stitch over 4 canvas threads that is at the bottom of the Double Leviathan Stitch. *See* Photo 2.

■ In Photo 1:
dark gray = light warm green
light gray = pinkish white

■ Do the light-green stitches first, then the pinkish white.

■ Start the first light-green Double Leviathan Stitch as indicated by the arrow in Photo 1, counting over

Photo 1. Framework of Patchwork I, Variation 1: Step 1. The armatures of the Double Leviathan Stitches.

Color Numbers and Amounts Needed
Patchwork I, Variation 1

Color	Approximate Amount	Colbert 6	Paterna
Deep red-violet	½ ounce	86	821
Medium red-violet	½ ounce	87	827
Light red-violet	½ ounce	88	828
Very light red-violet	1 ounce	89	831
Sherbet pink	2 ounces	178	865
Deep cool green	¼ ounce	129	559
Medium cool green	¼ ounce	131	G64
Light warm green	1 ounce	117	G74
Pinkish white	1 ounce	101	870
White	½ ounce	174	005

Plate 3. Patchwork I, Variation 1.

24 boxes from the left and starting the stitch in the 8th box down from the top.

- Photo 1 shows how your canvas will appear after you have completed Step 1.

Step 2

Go back and complete each one of those Double Leviathan Stitches. Use 2-ply yarn.

- Photo 3 shows how your canvas will appear after you have completed Step 2.

Step 3

Fill in each diagonal row within the framework of Double Leviathan Stitches. To do this, you will use (1) the Tent Stitch in squares of 4 stitches by 4 stitches, (2) the Scotch Stitch over 4 canvas threads, and (3) the Double Leviathan Stitch. Use 2-ply throughout.

- Photo 4 shows how your canvas will appear after you have completed one diagonal row.

Step 4

Add 4 rows of Tent Stitching all around the design in the appropriate colors, for the upholsterer's seam allowance.

COORDINATING DESIGN
Mountain Peaks, Variation 2 (Color Plate 16).

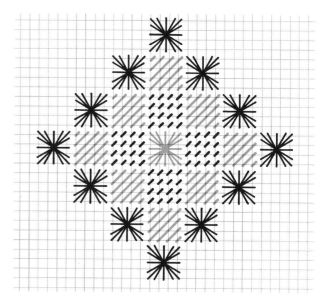

Fig. 2*. Stitch Pattern used for Patchwork I.

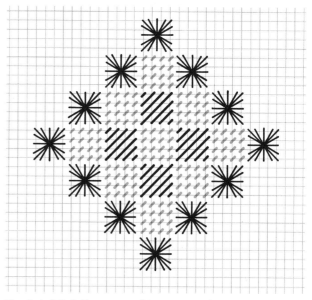

Fig. 2a*. Stitch Pattern used for Patchwork I, Variation 1.

Fig. 1*. Stitch Pattern used for Patchwork I.

Photo 2. Closeup of the armatures of the Double Leviathan Stitches.

Photo 4. One diagonal row of Patchwork I, Variation 1, filled in: Step 3.

Photo 3. The framework of Patchwork I, Variation 1: Step 2. The Double Leviathan Stitches completed.

Plate 4. Detail of Patchwork I, Variation 1.

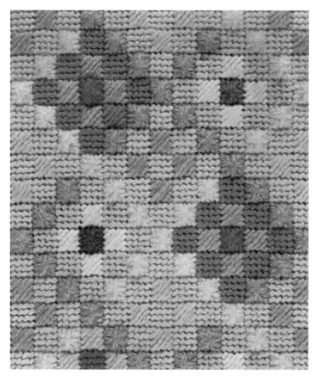

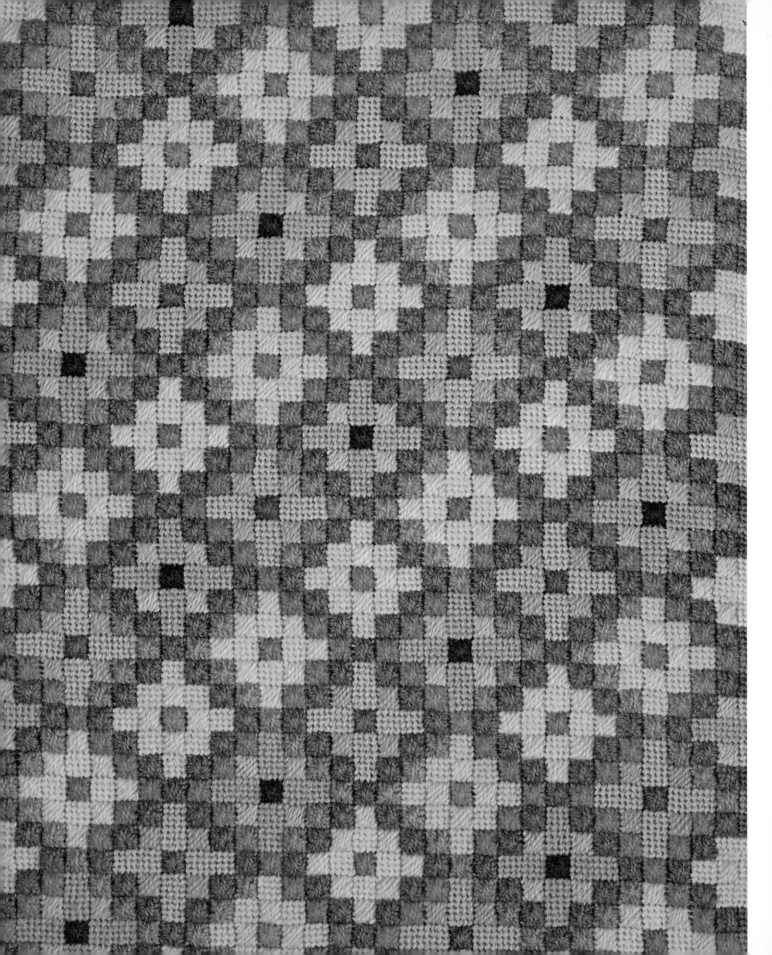

VARIATION 2

Step-by-Step Directions

[Color Plates 5 and 6]

MATERIALS:

No. 12 mono canvas
Persian yarn

DIMENSIONS:

15¾ x 12 inches
180 canvas threads by 132 canvas threads (includes 4 threads for seam allowance all around design)

STITCHES	ILLUSTRATIONS
Tent Stitch	Figs. 5a, 5b, 5c, 5d, 5e
Double Leviathan Stitch	Figs. 4a, 4b, 4c, 4d, 4e
Scotch Stitch over 4 canvas threads	Figs. 8a, 8b

Work from Color Plate **5** to follow the stitch pattern and color scheme. Figs. 1*, 2*, and 3* show the three stitch patterns used in this design.

Step 1

Set up the framework of the design by counting out and stitching the armatures of the Double Leviathan Stitches that are connected to one another. Use 2-ply yarn.

■ Photo 2 is a closeup of the armature. As explained on page 8, the armature of the Double Leviathan Stitch is the basic Cross Stitch over 4 canvas threads that is at the bottom of the Double Leviathan Stitch.

■ In Photo 5:

black = olive green
medium gray = light medium blue
light gray = tan

■ Do the olive green stitches first, then the blue, and then the tan.

■ Start the first olive green stitch as indicated by the arrow in Photo 5, counting over 20 boxes from the left and starting the stitch 8 boxes down from the top.

■ Photo 5 shows how your canvas will appear after you have completed Step 1.

Photo 5. The framework of Patchwork I, Variation 2: Step 1. The armatures of the Double Leviathan Stitches.

Color Numbers and Amounts Needed
Patchwork I, Variation 2

Color	Approximate Amount	Colbert 6	Paterna
Olive green	2½ ounces	27	553
Light medium blue	2 ounces	52	754
Tan	2 ounces	172	466
Lemon yellow	1 ounce	140	Y58
Gold-yellow	1 ounce	56	441
Sherbet pink	1 ounce	178	865
Light medium violet	1½ ounces	97	652
Very light blue-violet	1 ounce	155	641
Turquoise	¼ ounce	123	738
Light royal blue	¼ ounce	84	741
Deep cool green	¼ ounce	129	559
Forest green	¼ ounce	108	528

Plate 5. Patchwork I, Variation 2.

Step 2

Go back and complete each one of those Double Leviathan Stitches. Use 2-ply yarn.

Step 3

Fill in each diagonal row within the framework of Double Leviathan Stitches. Start with a yellow row, then do a violet row, and so on, alternating the color rows. The stitches used will be (1) the Tent Stitch in squares of 4 stitches by 4 stitches, (2) the Scotch Stitch over 4 canvas threads, and (3) the Double Leviathan Stitch. Use 2-ply yarn throughout.

Step 4

Add 4 rows of Tent Stitching all around the design in the appropriate colors, for the upholsterer's seam allowance.

COORDINATING DESIGN:
Lattice Work, Color Version 2 (Color Plate 10).

Plate 6. Detail of Patchwork I, Variation 2.

Fig. 3*. Stitch Pattern used for Patchwork I, Variation 2.

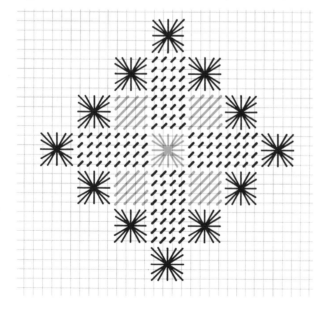

How to Do the Stitches and How They Can Be Combined

The Double Leviathan Stitch (shown in Figs. 4a, 4b, and 4c) is basically a Cross Stitch worked over 4 horizontal and 4 vertical canvas threads. Use 2-ply yarn on No. 12 canvas and 3-ply yarn on No. 10 canvas. I call the basic Cross Stitch (Steps 1, 2, 3, 4 in Fig. 4a) the *armature* of the Double Leviathan Stitch.

Then layers are built up over the armature as in Fig. 4b.

Fig. 4c shows Tent Stitching around a Double Leviathan Stitch.

Once you understand the construction of the Double Leviathan Stitch, it is easy to see that you can change the numbering according to the circumstances. For an example, see Figs. 4d and 4e. In my opinion, flexibility in the sequence of executing a stitch applies to many needlepoint stitches.

When doing the Double Leviathan Stitch I prefer not to scoop my needle. To scoop means to execute the down-and-up part of each stitch in one movement

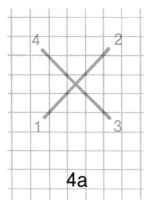

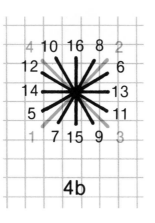

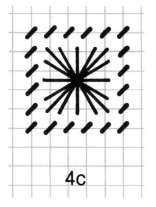

THE DOUBLE LEVIATHAN STITCH:

Fig. 4a. The armature of the Double Leviathan Stitch.
Fig. 4b. The Double Leviathan Stitch completed.
Fig. 4c. The Double Leviathan Stitch surrounded by Tent Stitches.

Fig. 4d, 4e. The Double Leviathan Stitch with different numbering.

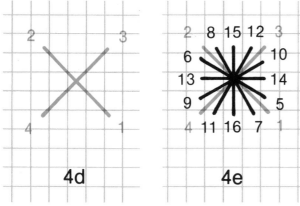

of the hand and needle.[1]* Instead, I like to do each of the stitches constituting the Double Leviathan Stitch in two movements of the hand. My needle is always at right angles to the canvas and goes down with one movement of the hand. Then I bring my hand to the back of the canvas and come up with another movement, still keeping the needle at right angles to the canvas. This traditional embroidery way of doing stitches is the preferable method for many of the fancy stitches on needlepoint canvas because it disturbs the threads of the canvas less than does scooping. For the same reason, I like to work on a frame, because this leaves both hands free to work, thus making it easy to keep the needle at right angles to the canvas. However, this is a personal preference, and it is best for you to decide for yourself whether to scoop or not to scoop.

The Tent Stitch shown in Figs. 5a through 5e is made with 2-ply on No. 12 and No. 14 and 3-ply on No. 10. The needle is scooped.

Fig. 5a shows the Tent Stitch done in the Continental manner, and Fig. 5b shows it done in the Basketweave fashion. I believe that one should be as flexible as possible in executing the Tent Stitch. Remember that it can be done in diagonal lines as shown in Fig. 5c, in vertical lines as in Fig. 5d, and also haphazardly for special shading effects as in Fig. 5e. Be sure to use the Basketweave method for large solid areas of Tent Stitching.

The Double Leviathan Stitch looks like a square piece of stone, a jewel, or a mosaic. That is why I call many designs using the Double Leviathan Stitch mosaic textures. The Double Leviathan Stitch inspires one to use it in patterns.

The Double Leviathan Stitch takes up a squared area on canvas and can be thought of as a square patch. Patches, or squares, can be put together in straight lines.

Fig. 6* (starred illustrations can be used as starting points for repeat designs) shows Double Leviathan Stitches in straight lines with Tent Stitching alongside. You see the armature and the armature built up.

* Notes begin on page 174.

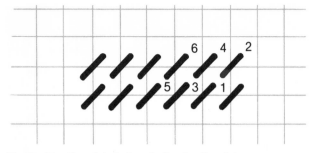

Fig. 5a. The Tent Stitch done in the Continental manner. (Detailed explanation on page 9.)

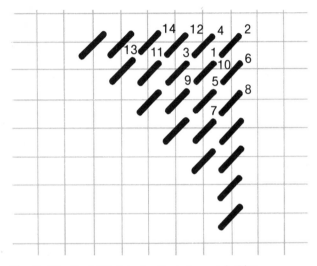

Fig. 5b. The Tent Stitch in the Basketweave fashion.

Fig. 5c. The Tent Stitch done in diagonal lines.

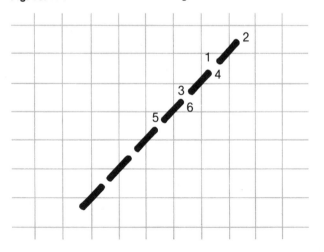

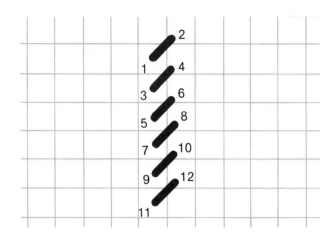

Fig. 5d. The Tent Stitch done in straight lines.

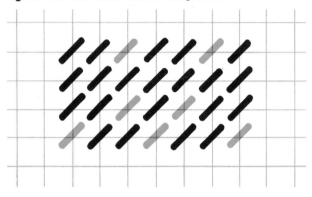

Fig. 5e. The Tent Stitch done haphazardly.

Do the armature of each stitch first. Then come back and build up each one.

The reason I emphasize doing the armature first is that if you should make a mistake in counting out or placing the stitches, it will show up. Once you get enough of the pattern set up you can easily check yourself by running your needle along the threads of the canvas to make sure the stitches are lined up correctly. If you have made a mistake, it is much easier to take out the armature or basic Cross Stitch than it is to remove the completed Double Leviathan Stitch.

After you have built up the Double Leviathan Stitches, fill in the Tent Stitches.

Patches or squares can also be placed in a diagonal line, but they have to be "stepped." That is, the diagonally opposite corners of the squares touch each other to form the steps.

Fig. 7* shows Double Leviathan Stitches stepped in two directions. *First do the armature of each Double Leviathan Stitch.* Then come back and build up the armature, completing each Double Leviathan Stitch. Then do the Tent Stitching.

Fig. 7* also shows that the space between the Double Leviathan Stitches breaks down into squares of 4 Tent Stitches by 4 Tent Stitches, or 16 Tent Stitches in a square.

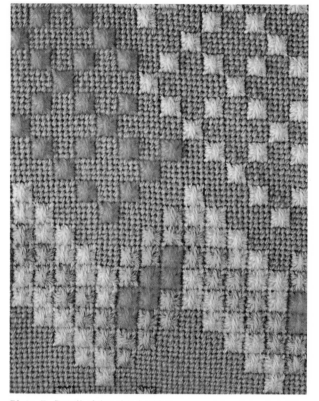

Plate 7. Detail of Jacob's Ladder.

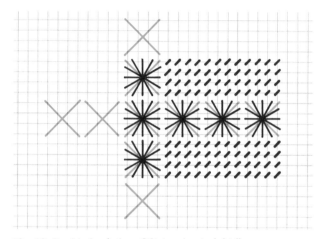

Fig. 6*. Double Leviathan Stitches in straight lines.

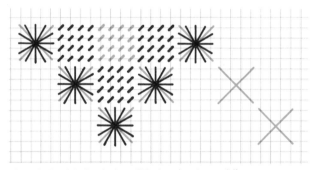

Fig. 7*. Double Leviathan Stitches in stepped lines.

Color Plate 7, a detail from Jacob's Ladder (see page 19 for step-by-step directions), shows how the Double Leviathan Stitch is used with the Tent Stitch to create an effective contrast of stitch quality. The Double Leviathan Stitch stands quite far out, and the Tent Stitching remains flat, providing a regular, bland and unobtrusive quality. The Tent Stitches look like pearls next to the mosaiclike, multifaceted Double Leviathan Stitches.

The textural contrast of the Double Leviathan Stitch and the Tent Stitch can be enhanced by introducing another texture, a soft one. "One of the most successful design contrasts is that of a sharp, crisp, or hard element, played against a soft element."[2] To facilitate integrating the stitches, the "soft" stitch must also be a square shape and cover the same number of canvas threads as the Double Leviathan Stitch. To achieve depth variation, this third element or stitch must not be as high as the Double Leviathan Stitch nor as flat as the Tent Stitch. I found what I was looking for in the Scotch Stitch over 4 canvas threads. (*See* Color Plate 6.)

Figs. 8a and 8b show the Scotch Stitch[3] over 4 canvas threads. Use 2-ply on No. 12 and No. 14 and 3-ply on No. 10. Fig. 8b shows the Scotch Stitch surrounded by Tent Stitches.

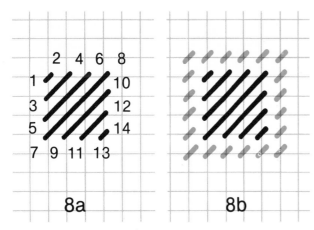

THE SCOTCH STITCH:

Fig. 8a. The Scotch Stitch over 4 canvas threads.
Fig. 8b. The same Scotch Stitch surrounded by Tent Stitches. (Detailed explanation starts on page 11.)

Fig. 9* shows that the Scotch Stitch over 4 canvas threads and the Double Leviathan Stitch each covers the same amount of canvas area.

The Scotch Stitch over 5 canvas threads (Fig. 10) is used in Robbing Peter to Pay Paul (Color Plate 18).

The Scotch Stitch is a good example of how one stitch can grow out of another. Basically, the Scotch Stitch is an expanded Mosaic Stitch, as shown in Figs. 11a and 11b. Fig. 11a shows the Mosaic Stitch and 11b the Scotch Stitch over 3 canvas threads.

The Double Leviathan Stitch and the Scotch Stitch done over 4 canvas threads are squared stitches of the same size. Since both stitches are square, you can do the same thing patternwise with Scotch Stitches that you can do with Double Leviathan Stitches.

Fig. 12* shows Scotch Stitches in straight lines; Fig. 13* shows them in stepped diagonal lines.

If you think of a 4-stitch by 4-stitch Tent Stitch square as a patch or a mosaic the same size as the Double Leviathan square and the Scotch Stitch square, combining them becomes just like putting identical-size pieces of square mosaic, or textured square patches, together.

Fig. 14* shows Tent, Scotch, and Double Leviathan Stitches in straight lines. Fig. 15* shows Scotch Stitches alternated with Double Leviathan Stitches in a checkerboard pattern.

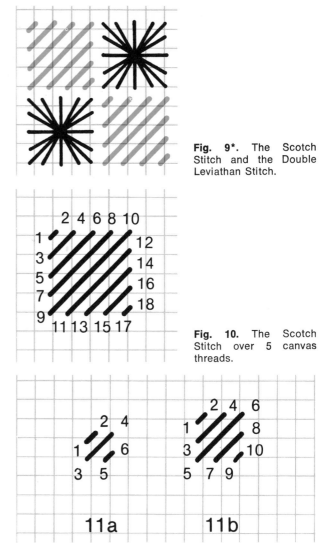

Fig. 9*. The Scotch Stitch and the Double Leviathan Stitch.

Fig. 10. The Scotch Stitch over 5 canvas threads.

Fig. 11a. The Mosaic Stitch.
Fig. 11b. The Scotch Stitch over 3 canvas threads.

Fig. 16* shows the 4-stitch by 4-stitch Tent Stitch squares that fit between alternated Double Leviathan and Scotch Stitches.

It is easy to integrate the Scotch, Double Leviathan, and Tent Stitches, because they are all basically slanting or diagonal stitches and are easily put into square shapes of the same size. You do not have to do any fudging or adding of little stitches to make these stitches fit into patterns.

Fig. 12*. Scotch Stitches in straight lines.

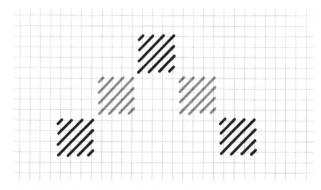

Fig. 13*. Scotch Stitches in stepped lines.

Fig. 14*. Tent, Scotch, and Double Leviathan Stitches in straight lines.

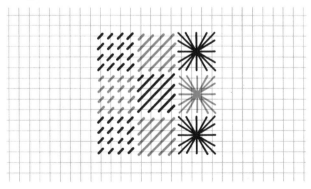

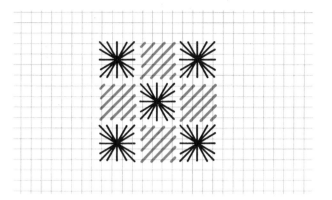

Fig. 15*. Scotch Stitches and Double Leviathan Stitches in a checkerboard pattern.

Fig. 16*. Tent Stitch squares in between alternated Double Leviathan and Scotch Stitches.

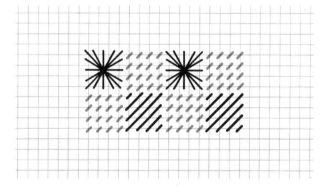

For Your Own Portfolio

Double Leviathan Stitches or squares can be put together in straight lines, blocks, checkered patterns, and grids. They can also be put together in diagonal stepped lines to create many interesting patterns.

Figs. 17* through 22* show mosaic textures using the Double Leviathan, Scotch, and Tent Stitches. These figures can be the bases for your own patterns and color designs. Remember—all starred figures can be starting points for repeat designs.

Fig. 17* shows the Double Leviathan and Tent Stitches used in a grid or checkerboard pattern. I have

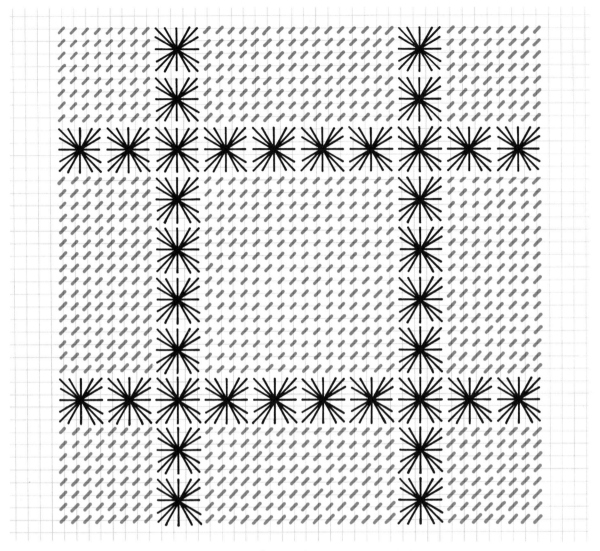

Fig. 17*. Mosaic Texture for your own portfolio: Double Leviathan and Tent Stitches in a grid or checkerboard pattern.

used this texture for a telephone book cover (*see* the acrylic study using an acetate overlay, Photo 40, page 114). Fig. 17* also allows for many variations, some studies for which are shown in Figs. 21* and 22*.

Fig. 18* shows Tent Stitching combined with Double Leviathan Stitches done in straight lines and Fig. 19*—which could be called Stepped Rectangles—in straight and stepped lines. Each rectangle consists of two squares.

Mosaic textures can be used for almost any type of needlepoint object. Photo 6 shows a belt, Night Sky, based on the textures shown in Figs. 1* and 2*.

The texture shown in Fig. 19* could be used for an evening bag, for which the Double Leviathan Stitches might be done in gold metallic thread.

Photo 7 shows my study for a belt or for a luggage strap in the King's Robe design. It was done on No. 14 mono canvas with 2-ply Persian yarn and double-strand gold metallic thread.

Fig. 20* illustrates a texture using Double Leviathan

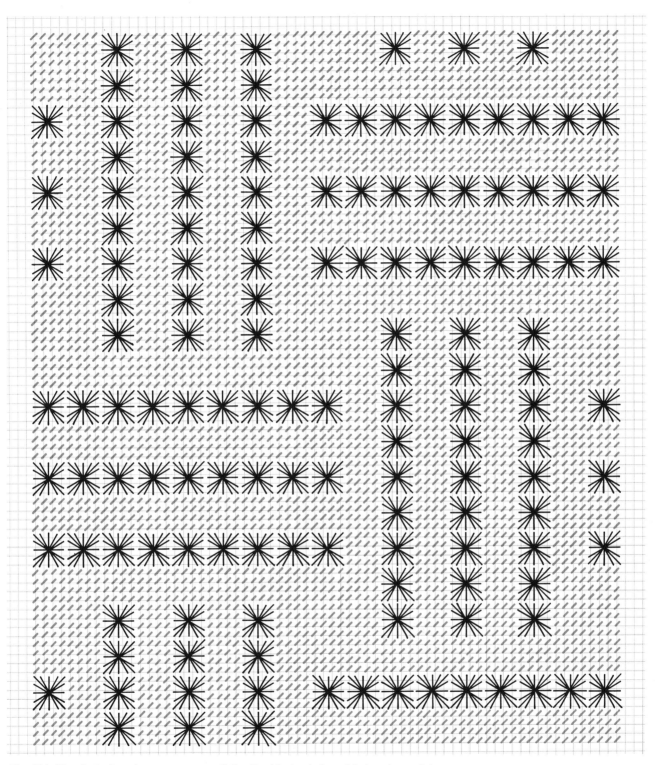

Fig. 18*. Mosaic texture for your own portfolio: Double Leviathan Stitches in straight lines combined with Tent Stitching.

Fig. 19*. Mosaic texture for your own portfolio: Stepped Rectangles using Double Leviathan and Tent Stitches.

Fig. 20*. Mosaic texture for your own portfolio.

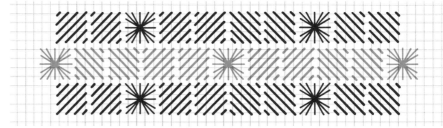

Fig. 21*. Freehand study for a mosaic texture.

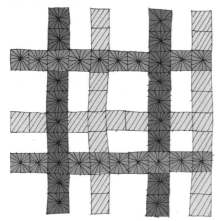

▓ Double Leviathan Stitch

▨ Scotch Stitch over four canvas threads

  Unmarked areas: Tent Stitch

▓ Double Leviathan Stitch

▨ Scotch Stitch over four canvas threads

  Unmarked areas: Tent Stitch

Fig. 22*. Freehand study for a mosaic texture.

Photo 6. Night Sky Belt.

Photo 7. Study for a belt or for a luggage strap in the King's Robe design.

Photo 8. Brick wall that inspired mosaic texture shown in Fig. 20.

and Scotch Stitches. Photo 8 shows the brick wall that inspired this texture.

A good way to work out your own mosaic designs is to make a freehand drawing in squares. Forget about the stitches—just make a pattern based on squares as in Figs. 21* and 22*. Both these drawings are based on the mosaic texture shown in Fig. 17*. (As a matter of fact, I traced over Fig. 17 to get the basic structure.)

Once you have drawn the freehand squares, you can easily superimpose with pen or pencil whatever stitches you wish to use. You will usually have several possibilities because a simple basic structure can be the starting point for many variations. The various grays used in Figs. 21* and 22* can stand for different colors. As these two illustrations demonstrate, it is not necessary to use graph paper to plan your designs. You can work directly from your freehand drawing when setting up your design on canvas.

If you want to be very professional, make the first sketch of the squares in color. Then use a piece of tracing paper or acetate as an overlay, and mark the stitches you will use on the overlay. If you want to try a different stitch combination, just use a fresh piece of tracing paper. In this way, you can try endless combinations without having to redo the original sketch of the squares. Photo 40 (page 114) shows one of my acrylic studies using an acetate overlay.

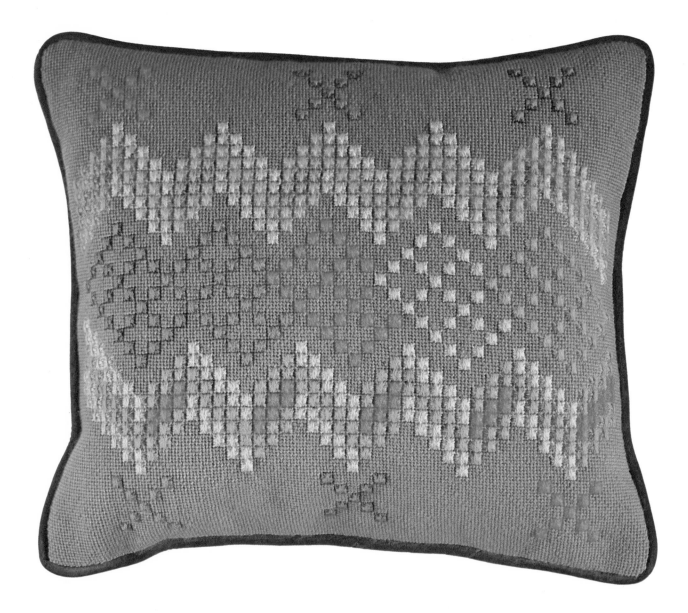

Plate 8. Jacob's Ladder

Jacob's Ladder

Step-by-Step Directions
[*Color Plates 7 and 8*]

MATERIALS:

No. 12 mono canvas

Persian yarn

DIMENSIONS:

14¾ x 17 inches

172 canvas threads by 188 canvas threads (includes 4 threads for seam allowance)

STITCHES	ILLUSTRATIONS
Tent Stitch	Figs. 5a, 5b, 5c, 5d, 5e
Double Leviathan Stitch	Figs. 4a, 4b, 4c, 4d, 4e

Work from Color Plate 8 to follow the stitch pattern and color scheme. The basic pattern used is the Double Leviathan Stitch used in stepped lines (Fig. 7*).

Step 1

Set up the framework of the design by counting out and stitching the armature of each Double Leviathan Stitch. Use 2-ply yarn.

- Start with the deep-orange X at top left of design.
- Start first deep-orange stitch as indicated by the arrow in Photo 9. Count over 16 boxes from the left and start the stitch in the 16th box down from top.
- After you have made the first deep-orange X, go directly beneath it to the next section of Double Leviathan Stitches. You will start with a light-turquoise Double Leviathan Stitch. Continue doing the various sections of Double Leviathan Stitches.
- Count out carefully the number of Tent Stitches that will fit between areas of Double Leviathan Stitches so you will know exactly where to start each section. Photo 9 shows the number of Tent Stitches between each section.
- Photo 9 shows how your canvas will appear after you have completed most of the work for Step 1.

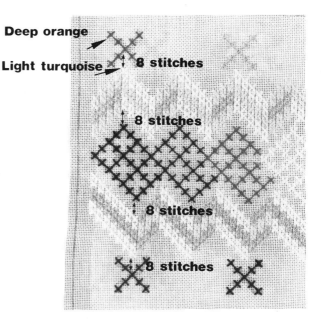

Photo 9. The armature framework of Jacob's Ladder.

Step 2

Go back and complete each of the Double Leviathan Stitches. Use 2-ply yarn.

Step 3

Fill background with Tent Stitching. Use 2-ply yarn.

COORDINATING DESIGN

Lattice Work, Color Version 1 (Color Plate 9).

Color Numbers and Amounts Needed Jacob's Ladder			
Color	Approximate Amount	Colbert 6	Paterna
Deep gold-orange (background)	9 ounces	35	427
Deep turquoise	1 ounce	122	728
Light turquoise	2 ounces	124	748
Deep yellow-green	1 ounce	90	545
Light yellow-green	2 ounces	91	550
Deep orange	1 ounce	125	960
Light orange	1½ ounces	128	975

Plate 9. Lattice Work, Color Version 1.

Lattice Work

Step-by-Step Directions

[*Color Plates 9 and 10*]

MATERIALS:

No. 12 mono canvas
Persian yarn

DIMENSIONS:

16 x 17½ inches
182 canvas threads by 192 canvas threads (seam allowance is not included)

STITCHES	ILLUSTRATIONS
Tent Stitch	Figs. 5a, 5b, 5c, 5d, 5e
Double Straight Cross Stitch	Fig. 30
Lattice Work Stitch	Figs. 25a, 25b, 25c, 25d

Work from Chart 1 for Color Version 1, or from Chart 2 for Color Version 2.

The Lattice Work Stitch is my own creation. I suggest that you read the detailed information about it and practice it before doing any designs with it. Besides Figs. 25a, 25b, 25c, and 25d, see Figs. 26, 27, 28, and 29.

Step 1

Set up the framework of the design by counting out and stitching the armature of the Lattice Work Stitches. Use 3-ply yarn.

■ The arrow in Photo 10 and the charts show where you should start your first stitch—in the first box at the upper left-hand corner.

■ In Fig. 23, the armature of the Lattice Work Stitch is shown with red lines and with numbers. Each straight stitch goes over 10 threads or 9 boxes.

■ Photo 10 shows how the armature framework of the design is set up on your canvas after you have completed Step 1.

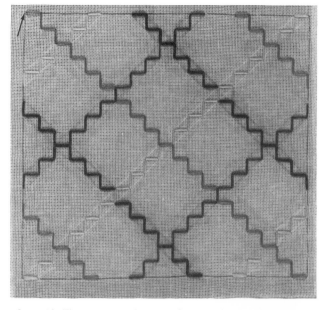

Photo 10. The armature framework of Lattice Work. Step 1.

■ You can count out the armature stitches on bare canvas as shown in Photo 11. Or you can paint the armature on canvas first, as shown in Photo 12. Be sure to use a permanent marking pen or a permanent paint —oil or acrylic.

Color Numbers and Amounts Needed Lattice Work, Color Version 1			
Color	Approximate Amount	Colbert 6	Paterna
Deep gold-orange	1 ounce	35	427
Light gold-orange	1 ounce	36	447
Deep orange	1 ounce	125	960
Medium orange	2 ounces	126	965
Light orange	1 ounce	128	975
Deep turquoise	1½ ounces	122	728
Light turquoise	2 ounces	124	748
Deep yellow-green	2 ounces	90	545
Light yellow-green	2 ounces	91	550

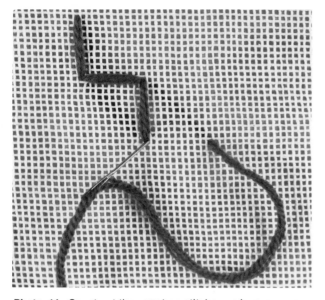

Photo 11. Count out the armature stitches on bare canvas.

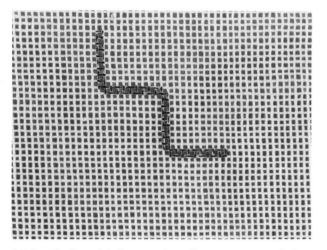

Photo 12. Or paint the armature lines on canvas before stitching.

Step 2

Fill in the Lattice Work Stitches. Use 3-ply yarn.

- This is shown in Fig. 23 with black lines and letters.
- Photo 13 shows how your canvas will appear when Step 2 is completed.
- Be sure to check the chart for correct color where bands overlap. *See* Fig. 28, page 27.

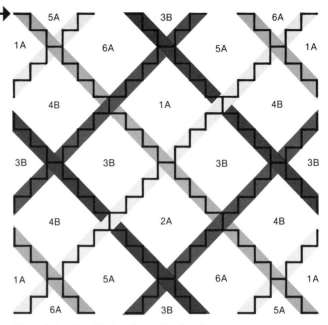

Chart 1. Lattice Work - Color Version 1

See Color Plate 9
Straight lines on chart indicate the armature of Lattice Work Stitch

Tones for Lattice Work Bands

☐ Light gold – yellow   ■ Medium orange

▨ Deep gold – yellow   ■ Deep orange

Colors and Stitches for Filling Diamonds

Color	1 – Medium orange	4 – Light turquoise
	2 – Light orange	5 – Deep yellow-green
	3 – Deep turquoise	6 – Light yellow-green

Stitch A – Double Straight Cross Stitch
B – Tent Stitch

**Color Numbers and Amounts Needed
Lattice Work, Color Version 2**

Color	Approximate Amount	Colbert 6	Paterna
Lemon yellow	2 ounces	140	Y58
Gold-yellow	4 ounces	56	441
Medium blue	½ ounce	51	752
Light medium blue	1 ounce	52	754
Very light blue	2 ounces	54	781
Violet white	2 ounces	99	011
White	2 ounces	174	005

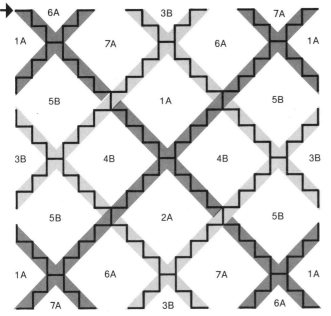

Chart 2. Lattice Work - Color Version 2

See Color Plate 10
Straight lines on chart indicate the armature of
Lattice Work Stitch

Tones for Lattice Work Bands

☐ Lemon yellow   ▨ Gold yellow

Colors and Stitches for Filling Diamonds

Color	1 - Gold-yellow	5 - Light blue
	2 - Lemon yellow	6 - White
	3 - Deep blue	7 - Violet white
	4 - Medium blue	

Stitch	A – Double Straight Cross Stitch
	B – Tent Stitch

Fig. 23. The Lattice Work Stitch in a diagonal band.

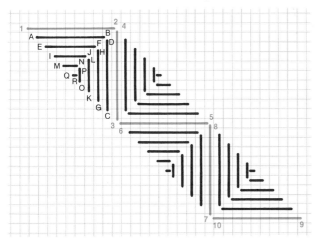

Photo 13. The framework of Lattice Work completed. Step 2.

Plate 10. Lattice Work, Color Version 2.

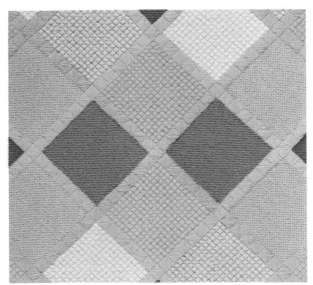

Step 3

Fill in the Double Straight Cross Stitch diamonds. Use 2-ply yarn.

- Fig. 24* shows how to center the first Double Straight Cross Stitch at the top part of the diamond.
- For filling in the whole diamond, see Fig. 34*, page 29.

Step 4

Fill in the Tent Stitch diamonds. Use 2-ply yarn.

- Figs. 24* and 29* show how to place Tent Stitches next to Lattice Work bands.

Step 5

Add a narrow seam allowance for the upholsterer. This can be done in Tent Stitching, a straight up-and-down stitch, or just a slight continuation of the stitches used in the design. Be sure to do the seam allowance in the appropriate colors.

COORDINATING DESIGNS
Color Version 1: Jacob's Ladder (Color Plate 8).
Color Version 2: Patchwork I, Variation 2 (Color Plate 5).

Fig. 24*. Centering the Double Straight Cross Stitch.

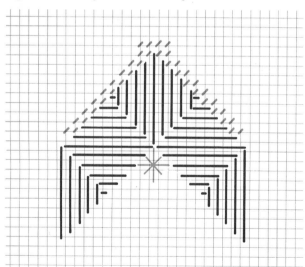

How to Do the Stitches and How They Can Be Combined

Figs. 25a and 25b show the Lattice Work Stitch. Use 3-ply on No. 12 and No. 14 and tapestry wool on No. 18. A straight up-and-down movement of the needle gives the best results; in other words, do not scoop the needle.

The armature of the Lattice Work Stitch is shown in red and with numbers in Fig. 25a. The armature consists of 2 straight stitches at right angles to each

THE LATTICE WORK STITCH STARTING WITH A HORIZONTAL STITCH

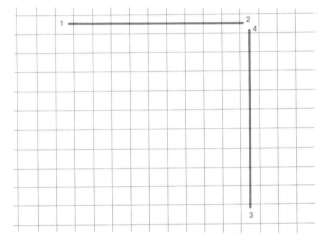

Fig. 25a. The armature of the Lattice Work Stitch.

Fig. 25b. The Lattice Work Stitch filled in.

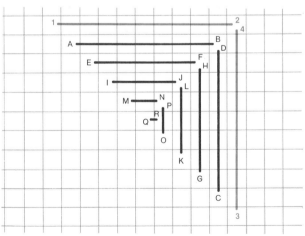

other, one vertical and one horizontal, each going over 10 canvas threads. Each of the armature stitches goes into the same hole at the right angle. Start the armature from the outer ends, as indicated by the numbers 1 and 3.

In Fig. 25b, the letters show how to fill in the Lattice Work Stitch. Remember: you have only to count over 9 boxes or over 10 threads when setting up the armature. To fill in, just make each successive pair of stitches one thread or one box smaller. Work from the outer ends, just as you did for the armature. When you fill in the Lattice Work Stitch, a right triangle is

formed. Notice that each right-angle stitch that you put in covers one thread fewer. One tiny little stitch is indicated by Q–R. You may or may not find it necessary to put this in.

Figs. 25c and 25d show that the Lattice Work Stitch can start with a vertical stitch as well as with a horizontal stitch as shown in Figs. 25a and 25b.

When doing the Lattice Work Stitch, it is preferable to use yarn that is approximately 70 inches long; that is, cut the skein only once. The stitch works up very quickly and to shorten yarn length means more frequent rethreading of the needle. With this stitch the long thread does not wear down, as so often happens with other stitches. Yarn length, however, is a matter of personal preference and each individual should do what suits himself best.

There are many ways in which Lattice Work Stitches can be used.

A diagonal band can be made (Fig. 26*). One side of the armature of each Lattice Work Stitch serves

THE LATTICE WORK STITCH STARTING WITH A VERTICAL STITCH

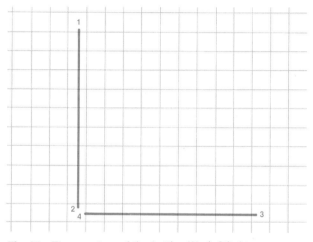

Fig. 25c. The armature of the Lattice Work Stitch.

Fig. 25d. The Lattice Work Stitch filled in.

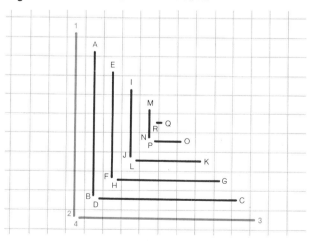

Fig. 26*. A diagonal band with the Lattice Work Stitch.

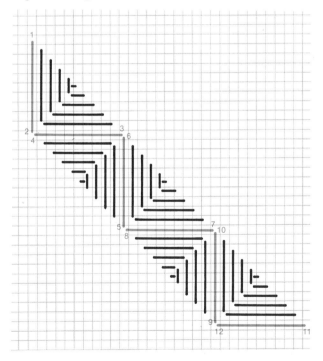

as part of the armature for the adjacent Lattice Work Stitch. Create the diagonal band by stitching in the armature of the whole band first, and then returning to fill in each stitch.

It is possible to change the direction in which the band slants (Fig. 27*).

You can overlap two diagonal bands that go in opposite directions, and thus achieve an X-shape (Fig. 28* and Color Plate 11). Intersect the bands at either a vertical or horizontal armature line. In Fig. 28*, the intersection is at a vertical armature line. In the color plate, the intersection is at a horizontal armature line. When you overlap two bands, notice that at the intersection you will fill in two halves of a Lattice Work Stitch—shown in the Figure by two arrows.

Fig. 29* shows how to put Tent Stitching next to a Lattice Work band. The Tent Stitch works well with the Lattice Work Stitch. Tent Stitching provides a flat, bland texture, and the stitches appear small in comparison to the larger stitches that make up the Lattice Work Stitch. Color Plate 11 shows the Tent Stitch next to the Lattice Work Stitch.

Fig. 30 shows the Double Straight Cross Stitch. Use 2-ply on No. 12 and No. 14, with a straight up-and-down movement of the needle. Do not scoop the needle.

The armature (Steps 1, 2, 3, 4) of the Double Straight Cross Stitch is an upright Cross Stitch over 4 canvas threads. The second layer (Steps A, B, C, D) is a diagonal Cross Stitch over 2 canvas threads. If 2-ply yarn is too thin for the canvas you are using, try using 3-ply for the first layer and 2-ply for the second layer.

As Fig. 31 shows, Double Straight Cross Stitches can be put in straight or diagonal lines. The diagonal lines can change direction (Fig. 32*).

Fig. 32* also shows that I suggest doing the armature first, then coming back to complete the second layer.

Fig. 27*. A Lattice Work Band can slant in opposite directions.

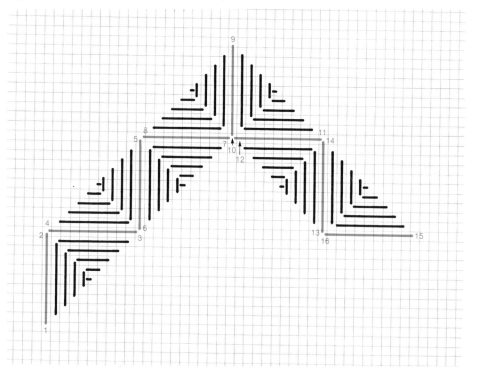

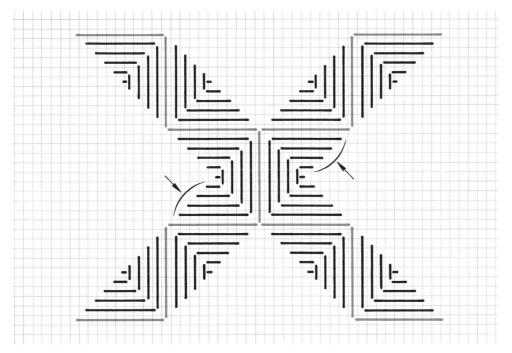

Fig. 28*. Overlapping bands of Lattice Work Stitches.

Fig. 29*. The Tent Stitch and the Lattice Work Stitch.

Plate 11. Detail of Lattice Work, Color Version 2.

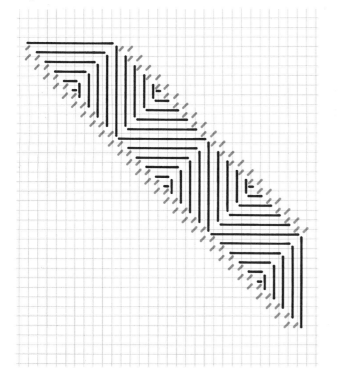

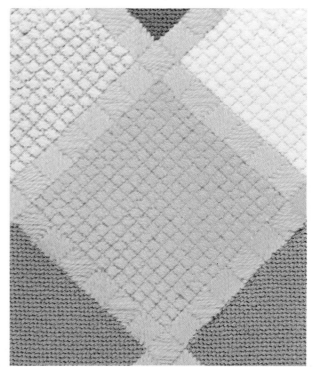

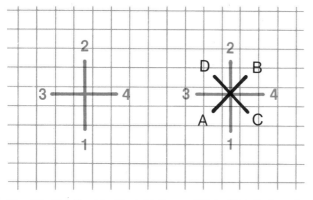

Fig. 30. The Double Straight Cross Stitch. (Detailed explanation starts on page 26.)

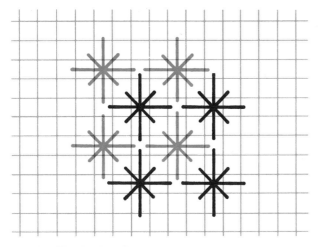

Fig. 31. The Double Straight Cross Stitch in straight and diagonal lines.

In Fig. 33*, Double Straight Cross Stitches are used in diamond shapes, and Fig. 34* shows them as a diamond inside of a diamond formed by Lattice Work bands.

The Double Straight Cross Stitch works well with the Lattice Work Stitch, providing a contrast of hard against soft. These two stitches integrate easily because both are based on horizontal and vertical stitches that can be easily put into diagonal directions or movements.

For Your Own Portfolio

The Lattice Work and Double Straight Cross Stitches can be used together to create quilted textures.

Fig. 35* shows how Lattice Work Stitches can be used to create a diamond shape by putting 4 stitches together back to back. Part of the armature of one stitch serves as part of the armature for another stitch.

Many interesting patterns can be made by combining the Lattice Work Stitch in diamonds and diagonal bands, either alone or with the Double Straight Cross Stitch. Some possibilities are shown in Figs. 36*, 37*, and 38*. Experiment with these stitches and have fun using them in various ways!

Fig. 32*. The Double Straight Cross Stitch can change direction of movement.

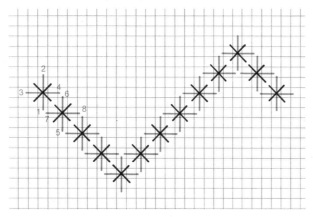

Fig. 33*. The Double Straight Cross Stitch in diamond shapes.

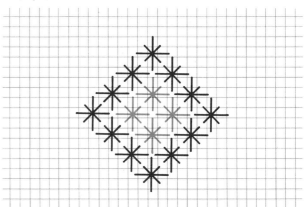

Fig. 34*. Double Straight Cross Stitches inside a diamond formed by Lattice Work bands.

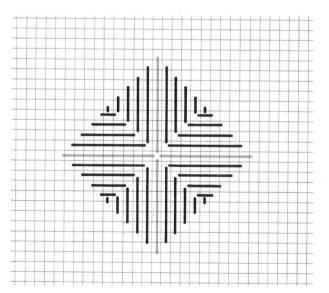

Fig. 35*. A diamond made with Lattice Work Stitches.

Fig. 36*. Quilted texture for your own portfolio.

Fig. 37*. Quilted texture for your own portfolio.

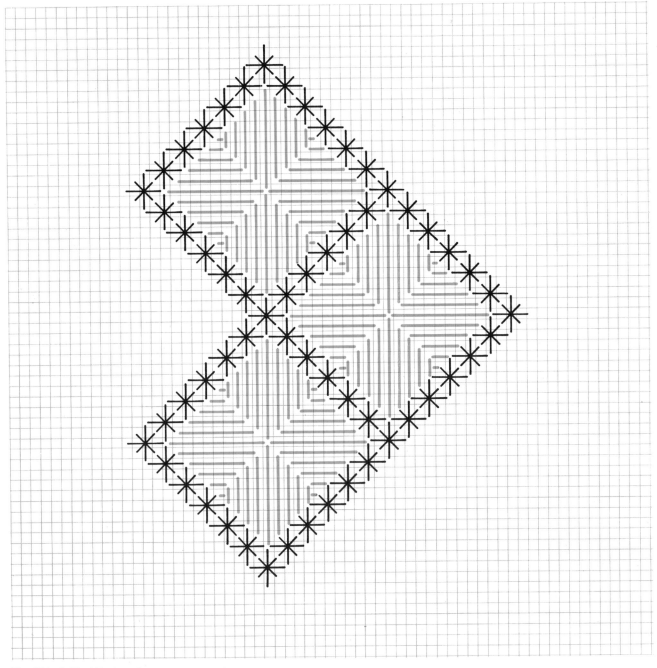

Fig. 38*. Quilted Texture for your own portfolio.

Tips on Making Up Patterns with Stitches

This section will help you to use the Figures as starting points for your own designs. It will also help you to use other stitches that you may know or may learn from other sources.

The first rule is to learn and understand in terms of structure and function the stitch or stitches you wish to use.

To familiarize yourself with the structure of a stitch, analyze it: Is it a diagonal stitch? If so, in what directions does it slant? Is it a vertical or horizontal stitch? Is it square or oblong or diamond-shaped? Is it built up in layers or is it a flat stitch? Can you find an armature for it?

Then, to understand the function of each stitch, ask: What can I do with it? What kinds of patterns can be made? Does it suit itself to squares? Does it suit itself to diagonals? Is it suitable for using in straight lines, and therefore for a linear pattern? Or is it good for filling out shapes—squares, rectangles, or diamonds?

To learn the answers to such questions you must spend some time experimenting with stitches. That is why I emphasize using practice canvas. As you determine how each stitch is constructed and understand its structure and function, try it out on various types of canvases with different kinds of wools. Then go on to experiment, to learn what other stitches that stitch can be used with. Thinking in terms of the structure and function of a stitch helps you to realize what will probably work well with it. This also helps you to conceive of an armature for the stitch.

One of the tricks to finding stitches that work well together is trying to see a common denominator in structure and function. For example, as previously pointed out, the Double Straight Cross Stitch integrates easily with the Lattice Work Stitch: Both stitches have armatures that go in horizontal–vertical directions—their structure is related. Both can be put easily into diagonal lines—their function is related.

The second rule in making up your own designs with stitches is to consider the whole design.

See if you can use a stitch to construct the framework of your design, as I did, for example, in the Lat-

Photo 14. Study for Lattice Work, Variation 2.

tice Work designs. Although I used the Lattice Work Stitch the least in the study shown in Photo 14, I emphasized it by using it to construct the framework or "lattice work" of the whole design. The finished piece is shown in Color Plate 38.

The Double Leviathan Stitch is used for the framework of Jacob's Ladder (Color Plate 8), Patchwork I (Color Plate 3), and Staircase Stripes (Color Plate 17). The diagonal function of the Lattice Work Stitch produces the composition of the Mountain Peaks designs as in Color Plate 13. I like to build my design as much as possible out of the structure and function of whatever stitch I am using.

If you wish to do your own designing, you have to be willing to try out ideas, make tentative decisions which you may or may not change, as you gradually build your entire design. That is why practice canvas is so useful. I make my mistakes on my practice canvas. Sometimes I just put in the armature of the stitch, though I may use the practice canvas to work out the eventual colors of a design. I indicate the colors and stitches boldly and as quickly as possible and concentrate on the visual unity of the design. A second piece of canvas is used for the finished work.

A third rule or guideline that will help you to design textured needlepoint is to use texture contrasts: *Hard against soft:* for example, Double Leviathan Stitch against the Scotch Stitch or Double Straight Cross Stitch against the Lattice Work Stitch. *Raised against flat:* the Double Leviathan Stitch against the Tent Stitch. *Shiny against matt:* the Lattice Work Stitch against the Tent Stitch. *Long against short:* for example, Lattice Work Stitch against the Tent Stitch.

In addition, it is possible to deepen the effect of textural contrast by being careful not to use two or three textures in equal amounts. In Lattice Work (Color Plate 9), the space allotted to the three different stitches is carefully varied: the Lattice Work Stitch is used the least amount, the Tent Stitch is used in the next largest amount, and the Double Straight Cross Stitch takes up the largest amount of space. I did this on purpose to make sure the amount of space each texture occupied would be clear.

If you are using two or three textures in a design, just make sure it is quite apparent which one is used the most, which one the least, and which one in an amount between those two extremes. It should be clear which texture dominates.[4] In fact, when you are using any design element, be it texture, color, shape, or pattern, don't repeat it evenly; vary it if at all possible. That's what gives visual interest.

Using Color Contrasts to Create the Pattern and Coordinate Two Pillows

In my work, I make consistent and conscious use of the fact that all the many colors in existence are derived from combinations of red, yellow, and blue, with possibly white or black added.

I do not necessarily paint studies for designs. I usually work directly with the wools and use my mind's eye to cross and mix colors. You can do the same when you design a piece of needlepoint. You don't have to paint it first, just be sure to try out the wools next to each other.

Very often, when choosing the colors for a design,

I start out with a small group of colors. Patchwork I, Variation 2 (Color Plate 5) and Lattice Work, Color Version 2 (Color Plate 10) are examples of how color knowledge was used in coordinating two pillows for a decorative interior.

My client wanted two pillows to go on a black divan in her front hall. She pointed out the colors among my stock of wools that were closest to the colors used in decorating her home. These were black, white, blue, yellow, and red.

We decided on the textures or stitch patterns that we would use—Patchwork and Lattice Work. My client has a tiled front hall in geometric diamond shapes, and we felt these would work well.

In Lattice Work, I kept the main color idea or scheme to contrasting the blue to the yellow and white.

Subsidiary, or within that, lemon yellow was contrasted with gold yellow. The original yellow that my client had shown me was a rather lemony and bluish yellow. In my mind's eye, I removed some of the blue or coolness, and thereby conceived of a yellow that was closer to orange, a golder and warmer yellow. Instead of saying I had removed the blue, you might say I had added a little red, or warmth, and therefore derived a goldish yellow. I like to compare cool and warm versions of the same color in one design.

I have sounded a chord in Lattice Work: blue, light blue, lemon yellow and gold yellow, and bluish white and pinkish white. I wanted in Lattice Work to make a clear color statement: "Look, here are blue and yellow and white, clearly side by side." (*See* pages 118–120 to learn how you can construct color chords for your designs.)

But then in the second pillow (Photo 15 and Color Plate 5) of this pair, I wanted to make a color statement that would be different and yet related. The Patchwork design, and this is one of the reasons for choosing it, does in fact allow for more color variation and orchestration, because there are so many more small parts that can be filled in with color. It was therefore easy to contrast and relate my color use in Patchwork to the color use in Lattice Work.

I decided to cross and mix the colors used in Lattice Work, see what would result, and then use the new colors, with some of the old, to construct the Patch-work pattern.

I asked myself: "What would happen if I mixed the blue and the yellow?" Why, of course, I would get green—so I started to look for greens that appealed to me to use in relation to the blues and yellows used.

Then I said to myself: "My client has red in her home. How am I going to get that into my Patchwork design?" I felt very strongly that introducing the strong primary red that she had selected would disrupt the poetic tonal unity that I was trying to produce in these two pillows. The red looked great in my client's home but, in these two pillows, it just didn't make sense to me to insert so vital and intense a red—it would appear foreign.

But I still felt that some stronger hint of red than that in Lattice Work, some redness, would be very useful in Patchwork. And so I mixed, in my mind's eye, red and blue, and started to look for violet shades. There is even a real pink in Patchwork, because I think of pink as red with white added to it.

Turquoise was put in because turquoise is a bluish form of green, and an olive green because olive is a yellowish form of green. I put in a tan because tan is a dull, or less intense, form of yellow.

I also decided that, to further contrast Patchwork to Lattice Work, I would not use either of the two whites used in Lattice Work. However, a slight feeling of whiteness is achieved by using pale or whitened shades of the violets.

It became apparent that the pattern of the Patch-work pillow could be constructed by contrasting violet to yellow, using turquoise and green in small amounts as accents. The pattern would have to bring out the contrast between violet and yellow.

I decided on a pattern of diagonal stripes, each row contrasting one to the other. You can see this design very clearly as being made up of diagonal stripes be-cause each diagonal stripe is either predominantly yellow or predominantly violet. There is a clear and obvious alternation of violet diagonal stripes and yel-low diagonal stripes.

Knowing about color contrasts and relationships is important because with that knowledge you are able to divide in an interesting way the space used in a de-

Plate 12. Study for Mountain Peaks Piano Bench.

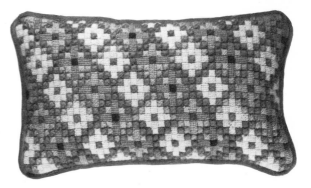

Photo 15. Pillow (8½ by 14½ inches): Patchwork I, Varia-tion 2. You can change the dimensions of the designs shown to suit your own needs.

sign. You want to make the sections of your design more clear or less clear, as you wish. That is how you construct a pattern.

By putting colors that are closely related to each other next to each other, you enliven the area through color variation, but you also allow your eye to see those sections more combined and together. When you put strongly contrasting colors, one next to the other, you demarcate those areas very clearly. You can make color work for you in bringing out the nature of your design—both as to its expressive or emotional quality as well as to its structural intent.

For more color information, see the Mini-Course in Color Fundamentals, which begins on page 107.

Mountain Peaks

VARIATION 1

Step-by-Step Directions

[*Color Plates 13 and 14*]

MATERIALS:

No. 14 mono canvas
Persian yarn

DIMENSIONS:

15½ x 12 inches
202 canvas threads by 162 canvas threads (seam
allowance is not included)

STITCH	ILLUSTRATIONS
Lattice Work Stitch	Figs. 25a, 25b, 25c, 25d

Work from Color Plate **13**. Fig. 39* and Fig. 40*
show the stitch pattern used in this design.

Step 1

Set up the Lattice Work Stitch armature of each
mountain peak row. Use 3-ply yarn.
- Start with the violet row. Count up from the bottom of the design 121 boxes and start your first stitch
in the 121st box.
- Photo 16 shows how your canvas will appear after
you have completed Step 1.

Step 2

Continue setting up the armature of mountain peak
row after mountain peak row.
- Photo 17 shows how your canvas will appear after
you have completed Step 2.
- The arrow in Photo 17 points to the first row, the
violet one, that you set up in Step 1.

Step 3

Fill in the Lattice Work Stitches in each mountain
peak row. Use 3-ply yarn.

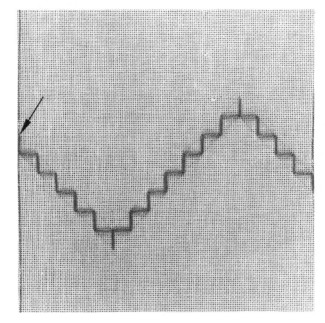

Photo 16. Mountain Peaks, Variation 1: Step 1.

**Color Numbers and Amounts Needed
Mountain Peaks, Variation 1**

Color	Approximate Amount	Colbert 6	Paterna
Sherbet pink	1 ounce	178	865
Medium red-violet	½ ounce	87	827
Light red-violet	½ ounce	88	828
Very light red-violet	1 ounce	89	831
Maroon	½ ounce	173	236
Medium violet	½ ounce	96	650
Light blue-violet	½ ounce	154	631
Very light blue-violet	½ ounce	155	641
Navy blue	½ ounce	175	305
Royal blue	½ ounce	82	731
Deep green-blue	½ ounce	133	763
Medium indigo blue	½ ounce	70	386
Deep turquoise	½ ounce	122	728
Deep cool green	½ ounce	129	559
Medium warm green	½ ounce	116	G64
Light warm green	1 ounce	117	G74
Olive green	½ ounce	27	553
Violet white	1 ounce	99	011

37

Plate 13. Mountain Peaks, Variation 1.

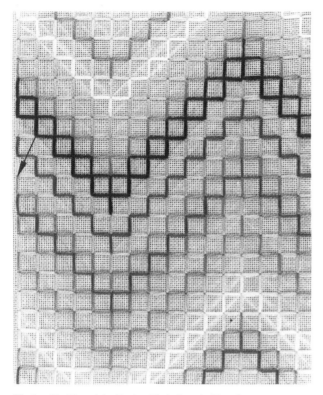

Photo 17. Mountain Peaks, Variation 1: Step 2.

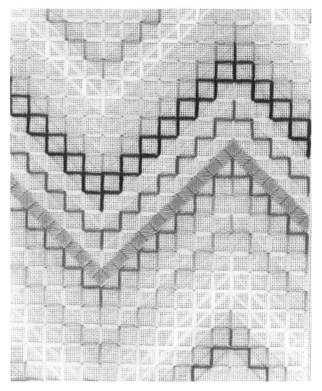

Photo 18. Mountain Peaks, Variation 1: Step 3.

■ Photo 18 shows how your canvas will appear after you have filled in one mountain peak row.

Step 4

Add a narrow seam allowance for the upholsterer. This can be done in a straight up-and-down stitch or just a continuation of the Lattice Work Stitches. Mountain Peak pillows are most effective when they are boxed with a coordinating color for the welting.

I have displayed Mountain Peaks, Variation 1, stretched on canvas stretchers and sitting on a small easel on a coffee table.

How to Do the Stitches and How They Can Be Combined

The Lattice Work Stitch is used to create a symbol for a mountain peak (Fig. 39* and Photo 19). The armature is shown in red, with numbers to indicate the order of working. Set up the entire armature first, and then go back and fill in each Lattice Work Stitch.

There are three sections to the mountain peak symbol: the peak or upside-down V at the right top, the valley or right-side-up V at the lower left, and the side of the mountain—the long diagonal band that joins the peak to the valley.

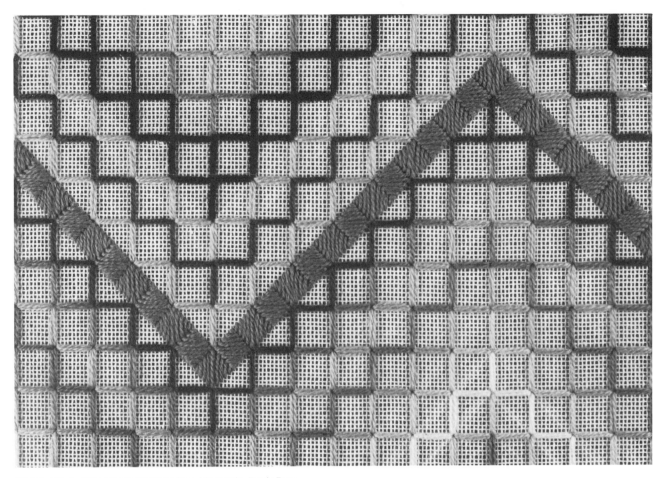

Photo 19. Lattice Work Stitches in a Mountain Peak Row.

Repeat mountain peak row after mountain peak row (Fig. 40*) until your whole canvas shape is filled out.

Two colors are used in this illustration to distinguish one mountain peak row from another. The black dots under the lines indicate the armature of the Lattice Work Stitching.

Set up the armature of each row first. Then go back and fill in each Lattice Work Stitch.

If you have done any traditional bargello designs, you will see that Mountain Peaks (Color Plate 13 and Photo 20) is designed in somewhat similar fashion.

Set up your first line or row, setting the pattern. Start the Mountain Peaks designs in the middle of the canvas and work from the middle out.

As you reach the lower right-hand corner of the canvas, you will be able to repeat only the symbol for the peak, and it will get smaller and smaller. As you reach the upper left-hand corner, you will be able to repeat only the symbol for the valley, and it, too, will get smaller and smaller.

In this design a distinct textural effect is achieved by using just one stitch alone. The softness of the Lattice Work Stitch predominates and the whole design has a soft, quilted feeling. The Lattice Work Stitch reflects light beautifully and automatically seems to make colors shine.

In Fig. 41* Double Straight Cross Stitching conforms to the shape of the Lattice Work Stitch moun-

Fig. 39*. The Lattice Work Stitch in a Mountain Peak Row.
(Detailed explanation on page 38.)

Fig. 40*. Mountain Peak Rows of Lattice Work Stitches repeated.
(Detailed explanation on page 39.)

Plate 14. Detail of Mountain Peaks, Variation 1.

Photo 20. Mountain Peaks, Variation 1.

tain peak row. A row of Double Straight Cross Stitching is between two Lattice Work rows. Red indicates the armature of the Lattice Work Stitches and the Double Straight Cross Stitches. Set up the entire armature of each of the rows first, then go back and fill in.

Although you can start the armature of the Lattice Work Stitches at the edge of the design, it is easier to start the armature of the Double Straight Cross Stitching at a mountain peak. This sequence is shown by the numbers and letters in Fig. 41*.

Fig. 42* shows three rows of Double Straight Cross Stitching in the mountain peak pattern. The Double Straight Cross Stitch gives a hard, incisive feeling against the softer, more diffused quality of the Lattice Work Stitch. Color Plate 15 is a detailed view of Mountain Peaks, Variation 2.

Using the same color but changing the stitch can make that color appear different, even if only slightly. This adds considerable visual interest. (*See* Color Plates 15 and 16.)

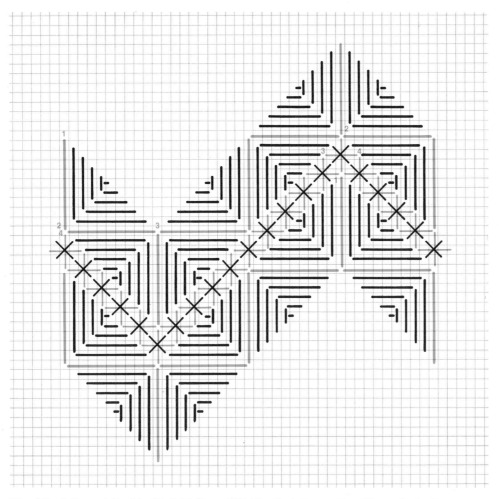

Fig. 41*. A Row of Double Straight Cross Stitching in between Two Mountain Peak Rows of Lattice Work Stitches. (Detailed explanation starts on page 39.)

For Your Own Portfolio

Color and Texture

Patterns can be built with stitches. A stitch may already be in a geometric shape, or you, as the designer, may put it into one. Then you can repeat the geometric shape in all sorts of patterns. Color can play an important role in bringing out pattern. There is a relationship between color use and textural effect.

In Mountain Peaks, Variation 1 (Color Plate **13**) a very simple repeat idea is used: constant repetition of

the mountain peak row. The textural effect and quality of this design are quite uniform. A more complex and stronger visual pattern emerges through color use and variation. Try to imagine this design all in one color. I think it would be quite boring, whereas a design such as Staircase Stripes (Color Plate **17**), where there is much more variation within the stitches used, might be quite interesting all in one color.

Both variations of Mountain Peaks are well suited for shading effects. However, the one which uses one stitch alone needs a greater number of colors, whereas the variation that is built on the use of two stitches

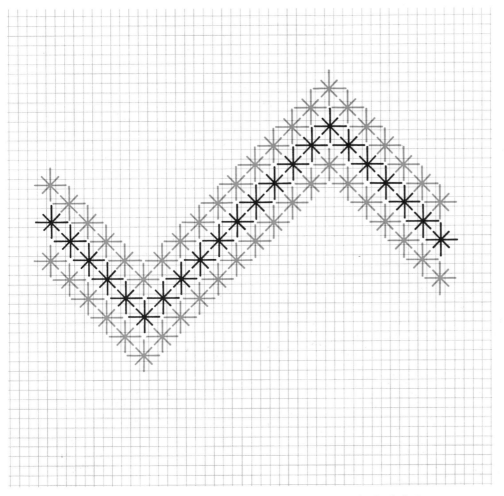

Fig. 42*. Three rows of Double Straight Cross Stitching in the Mountain Peak Pattern.

needs a smaller number of colors.

When you design with just one stitch, you can use more colors than if you are designing with many stitches. If you limit your design to one stitch alone, to bring out the textural effect and make the design more visually interesting, you must use a wide color range.

The less contrasting texture I use, the more color variation I use. Conversely, the more texture, in general, the less color variation is needed. Color variation in this context means the number of colors used. It does not mean shading effects. However, on occasion,

I have not hesitated to break this rule as in Robbing Peter to Pay Paul (Color Plate 18), Byzantine Jewels, No. 3 (Color Plate 21), and Cat Pillow (Color Plates 26 and 27).

If you are fearful of your ability to use and handle color, or if you fear you get mixed up with too many colors, or if, for decorative reasons, you don't want to put a lot of color into one piece, choose designs that emphasize texture contrast and stitch variation.

However, even if you are fearful of color, try Mountain Peaks just for the fun of it! Don't worry about what you will do with it—just play with color in this

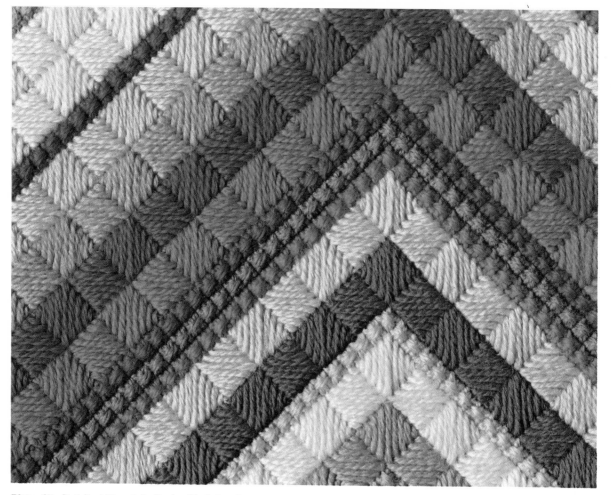

Plate 15. Detail of Mountain Peaks, Variation 2.

piece—do all the things you would never dare to do—even if you never show it to anybody. I am willing to bet that, after doing that, you will be less fearful of color. You might even find you are quite pleased with yourself!

If you love color and want to use it in an effective and expressive way, Mountain Peaks is an excellent choice. I never tire of doing color versions of Mountain Peaks. Its structure gives me a chance to use many colors, get all kinds of effects and feelings, and I find it very relaxing.

The colors for one version of Mountain Peaks were chosen after I had spent a summer designing the Staircase shown in Color Plate 48. For that design, a simple color scheme had been selected as appropriate for the decorative interior. If I work with only a few colors for a long period of time, I really want to use the ones I have disciplined myself to give up.

And so, I took all the leftovers—the warms, the cools, the lights, and the darks of the colors in the Staircase, the colors I had tried out and loved but rejected for the sake of the greater unity of the Staircase—and just had a great time putting them together. Stepchildren colors *can* be put together. As a matter of fact, the same thing happened, as far as the colors are concerned, with Mountain Peaks, Variation 1 (Color Plate 13) and Byzantine Jewels, No. 3 (Color Plate 21). These two designs employ the unused colors from a commission for six dining-room chair seats.

Breaking the Pattern with Color and Stitch Use

Mountain Peaks, Variation 2 (Color Plate 16), is based on alternating mountain peak rows of Lattice Work and Double Straight Cross Stitches. The design could have been simply built by repeating one row of Lattice Work Stitches and then one row of Double Straight Cross Stitches as suggested in Fig. 41*, page 44. This would have been a simple 1–2 repeat. Instead, I broke that pattern with color and stitch use.

In most instances one row of Double Straight Cross Stitching is used between two or more rows of Lattice Work Stitches. Mountain peak rows of Lattice Work Stitches are used to create larger and smaller intervals between the rows of Double Straight Cross Stitching. Because of the larger and smaller intervals, the design develops a rhythm. And as a result, the thin hard line of the Double Straight Cross Stitching stands out against the wider and softer bands of Lattice Work Stitches. The effect is not boring, expected or wasted. One of the surest ways to emphasize a visual element, be it a color, a texture, or a shape, is to use it sparingly in relation to another element, which you use in a larger amount.

In one part of the design, I used three rows of Double Straight Cross Stitching, instead of just one. This variation makes the design more interesting. The Double Straight Cross Stitching had been emphasized by isolating it against the Lattice Work background; now I focused on the Double Straight Cross Stitching by putting three rows together in one part of the design.

In other words, I set the pattern, a repetition of rows of Lattice Work Stitches in a mountain peak pattern, interrupted occasionally by single rows of Double Straight Cross Stitching in the same pattern. Then I broke the pattern, by putting in three rows of Double Straight Cross Stitching. (*See* Color Plate 16.)

I also broke the pattern with color use.

In all the Mountain Peaks designs shading is used in an abstract way. Shading effects—that is, the glowing effects that come of putting colors of differing lightness and darkness next to each other—can be used just for their sake alone, just to enrich any type of visual design, and hopefully, to contribute to its total unity, effect, and expressiveness. Shading in needlepoint does not have to relate to any object in our environment. It can just be done for its sheer beauty.

In Mountain Peaks, Variation 2 (Color Plate 16), I have used various shades of pink, from the deep red-violet to the light red-violet, to the sherbet pink and pinkish white. I did not limit myself to the tones or shades of one pink family, choosing instead pinks from three color families, using in some places a warmer pink and other places a cooler pink. And then to really set off and accent the pinks, a very opposite color—green—is used in a relatively smaller amount. The shading effect is concentrated in the center of the design, leaving relatively unshaded areas at the upper left and lower right. This is done on purpose to create a dominant area in the design and thus create visual variety and interest.

Technically, Mountain Peaks is a repeat pattern: the same movement is repeated over and over again—a linear or flat symbol for a mountain peak. It is possible to de-emphasize the repeat nature of the pattern, to a greater or lesser degree, by color, texture, and interval variation. Breaking the pattern makes the eye see something other than a 1–2 repeat.

I like to make a repeat design look like a nonrepeat. Another example of this approach is Robbing Peter to Pay Paul (Color Plate 18). I try to discover a new unity when I am using a repeat, to create a whole total unity with all the means at my disposal. And if an insistent repetitious pattern develops, very often, though not always, I try to break it.

VARIATION 2

Step-by-Step Directions

[*Color Plates 15 and 16*]

MATERIALS:
No. 14 mono canvas
Persian yarn

DIMENSIONS:
14½ x 11¾ inches
204 canvas threads by 162 canvas threads (seam allowance is included)

STITCHES	ILLUSTRATIONS
Lattice Work Stitch	Figs. 25a, 25b, 25c, 25d
Double Straight Cross Stitch	Fig. 30

Work from Color Plate **16** to follow the color and stitch pattern. Fig. 41* (page 44) and Fig. 42* (page 45) show the stitch patterns used in this design.

Step 1

Set up the Lattice Work Stitch armature of the deep red-violet mountain peak row. Use 3-ply yarn.

- Count up from the bottom of the design 111 boxes and start your first stitch in the 111th box.
- The arrow in Photo 21 points to the first row, the deep red-violet one, that you should set up. (*See* page 50.)

Step 2

Work from that row outward on either side, doing whatever comes next—the armature of a mountain peak row of Lattice Work Stitching or the armature of a mountain peak row of Double Straight Cross Stitching.

- Start the Double Straight Cross Stitch row as shown enlarged in Photo 22. (*See also* Fig. 41.)
- Remember to use 2-ply yarn for the armature of the Double Straight Cross Stitch.

- To repeat: At this point you should only be setting up the armatures. You should not yet be filling in or completing the stitches.
- Photo 21 shows how your canvas will appear after you have completed Steps 1 and 2.

Step 3

Now go back and complete each stitch in each of the rows, either filling in the Lattice Work Stitches or doing the top layer of the Double Straight Cross Stitching.

- Photo 18 (page 38) will give you an idea of how your canvas will look after you have filled in one Lattice Work row.

Step 4

Add a narrow seam allowance for the upholsterer. This can be most easily done as a continuation of the stitches of the design. Mountain Peak pillows are most effective when they are boxed with a coordinating color for the welting.

COORDINATING DESIGN
Patchwork I, Variation 1 (Color Plate **3**)

Color Numbers and Amounts Needed
Mountain Peaks, Variation 2

Color	Approximate Amount	Colbert 6	Paterna
Deep red-violet	1 ounce	86	821
Medium red-violet	1 ounce	87	827
Light red-violet	1½ ounces	88	828
Sherbet pink	2 ounces	178	865
Deep cool green	1 ounce	129	559
Medium warm green	½ ounce	116	G64
Light warm green	1 ounce	117	G74
White	3 ounces	174	005

Plate 16. Mountain Peaks, Variation 2.

Photo 21. Armature framework of Mountain Peaks, Variation 2.

Photo 22. Closeup of starting the Double Straight Cross Stitch within a mountain peak of Lattice Work Stitches.

Plate 17. Staircase Stripes used for a telephone book cover.

Staircase Stripes

TELEPHONE BOOK COVER

Step-by-Step Directions

[*Color Plate* 17]

MATERIALS:

    No. 12 mono canvas
    Persian yarn

DIMENSIONS:

    10¾ x 8¾ inches (needlepoint)
    12 x 10 inches (finished with leather)
    128 canvas threads by 100 canvas threads (seam allowance is not included)

STITCHES	ILLUSTRATIONS
Double Leviathan Stitch	Figs. 4a, 4b, 4c, 4d, 4e
Tent Stitch	Figs. 5a, 5b, 5c, 5d, 5e
Byzantine Stitch over	
2 canvas threads	Figs. 43*, 43a, 43b
Diagonal Parisian Stitch	Figs. 44*, 44a
Diagonal Hungarian Ground	Figs. 45*, 45a

If your telephone book measures 11 x 9 inches make your needlepoint piece 10¾ x 8¾ inches for mounting with a leather border and leather back cover. Be sure to check the exact size of your telephone book and make any necessary adjustments. Modern Needlepoint Mounting Company, 11 West 32 Street, New York, New York 10001, mounts telephone book covers. Be sure to provide them with the exact dimensions of your telephone book, including the thickness of the book.

Work from Color Plate **17** and Photo 23 to follow the stitch pattern and color scheme.

Step 1

Set up the framework of the design by counting out and stitching the armature of each Double Leviathan Stitch. Use 2-ply yarn.

- Start with the very deep royal blue staircase stripe at the upper left of the design.
- Start the first Double Leviathan Stitch as indicated by the arrow in Photo 23, counting over 8 boxes from the left and starting the stitch 12 boxes down from the top.
- Each staircase stripe of Double Leviathan Stitches on the left-hand side of the design starts out with 4 Double Leviathan Stitches in a vertical column. Each of these vertical columns is 4 threads apart on the left-hand side of the design.
- Each staircase stripe of Double Leviathan Stitches on the right-hand side of the design ends up with a horizontal row of 3 Double Leviathan Stitches. The space between the last Double Leviathan Stitches in these rows measures 16 threads.
- As you set up each staircase stripe of Double Leviathan Stitches, count carefully on the sides of the design the number of canvas threads between each Double Leviathan Stitch that starts a new staircase stripe. This is important because you want to know exactly where to start your next staircase stripe, and you want the design to fill out the dimensions properly. Photo 23 shows the number of canvas threads between the staircase stripes of Double Leviathan Stitches.

Color Numbers and Amounts Needed
Staircase Stripes, Telephone Book Cover

Color	Approximate Amount	Colbert 6	Paterna
Deep blue-green	2 ounces	147	718
Light turquoise	1 ounce	124	748
Very deep royal blue	1 ounce	80	721
Light medium			
warm green	2 ounces	113	574
Deep olive green	½ ounce	26	540
Deep red-violet	½ ounce	86	821

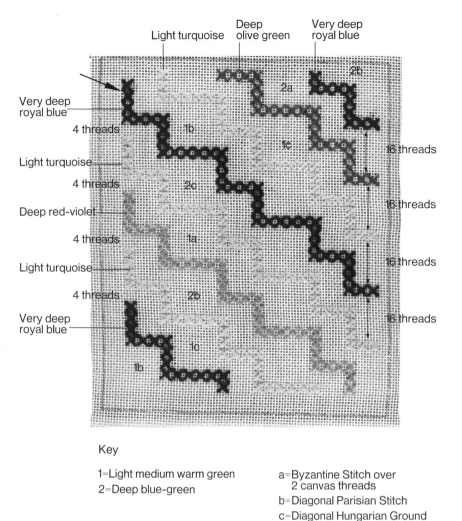

Key

1=Light medium warm green
2=Deep blue-green

a=Byzantine Stitch over
    2 canvas threads
b=Diagonal Parisian Stitch
c=Diagonal Hungarian Ground

Photo 23. Armature framework of Staircase Stripes.

■ Photo 23 shows how your canvas will appear after you have completed Step 1.

Step 2

Complete each Double Leviathan Stitch. Use 2-ply yarn.

Step 3

Do the areas between the Double Leviathan Stitches in the appropriate colors and stitches. You will do (1) the Byzantine Stitch over 2 canvas threads, (2) the Diagonal Parisian Stitch, and (3) the Diagonal Hungarian Ground. Use 2-ply yarn throughout. Photo 23 identifies the fillings by name and indicates the colors to be used.

■ NOTE: After starting each filling up against one inside corner of Double Leviathan Stitches, continue each filling, counting out the stitches carefully so you are able to set up the pattern as if it were not blocked by Double Leviathan Stitches. This method was not completely followed in the piece shown in Color Plate **17.**

Step 4

Fill out the remaining area of the design with Tent Stitching in the appropriate colors. Make sure you add on an extra 3 rows of Tent Stitching for the mounter's seam allowance. Use 2-ply yarn.

How to Do the Stitches and How They Can Be Combined

Photo 24 is a detail of Staircase Stripes (shown in Color Plate 17), with the names of the stitches given.

Each filling used in Staircase Stripes is shown up against the inside corner or step of Double Leviathan Stitches.

Fig. 43* shows the Byzantine Stitch over 2 canvas threads.

Fig. 44* shows the Diagonal Parisian Stitch.

Fig. 45* shows the Diagonal Hungarian Ground.

For all three fillings, use 2-ply yarn on No. 12 canvas. Scoop the needle.

The red stitches used in these three figures indicate the fudging stitches that are needed to square off each filling.

Doing these fillings, I try to start each diagonal row *with the stitches that are shown circled* so that the alternating pattern is easy to set up. It is preferable to work in relation to something that is clearly established, instead of counting to the top or bottom of each successive diagonal row.

Figs. 43*, 44*, and 45* each have accompanying figures showing the fillings by themselves. Fig. 43a, for example, shows the Byzantine Stitch over 2 canvas threads with the standard numbering. Fig. 43b shows it with the numbering I prefer. In Figs. 43a, 43b, 44a, and 45a two colors are used so that you can see clearly how the fillings are worked in diagonal rows.

Fig. 44a gives my numbering for the Diagonal Parisian Stitch and Fig. 45a gives it for the Diagonal Hungarian Ground.

The only disadvantage to my numbering method is that you will have some loose thread on the back of your canvas as you skip around. I usually weave the thread in and out of the stitches already made on the back and carry the thread to whatever part I wish to work. The extra wool on the back of the canvas is an advantage. It does not make the fabric too bulky, and it does make it stronger.

Photo 24. Detail of Staircase Stripes.

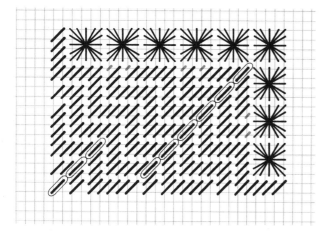

Fig. 43*. Byzantine Stitch over 2 canvas threads and Double Leviathan Stitches.

Fig. 43a. Byzantine Stitch by itself with the usual numbering. (Detailed explanations for these fillings on page 55.)

Fig. 43b. Byzantine Stitch by itself with my numbering.

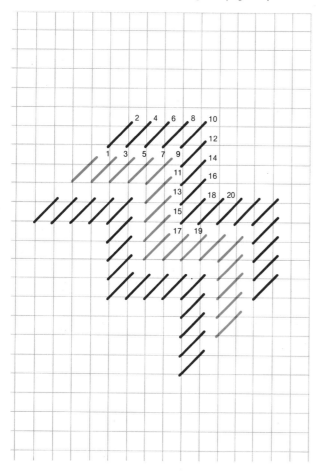

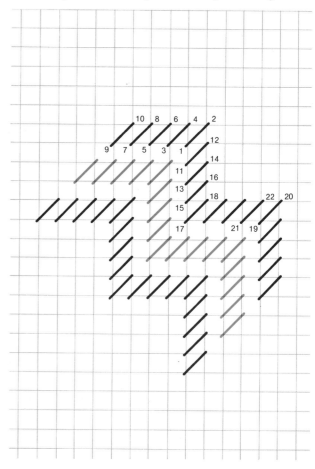

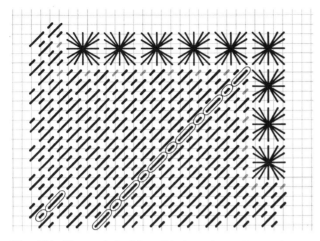

Fig. 44*. Diagonal Parisian Stitch and Double Leviathan Stitch.

Fig. 45*. Diagonal Hungarian Ground and Double Leviathan stitches.

Fig. 44a. Diagonal Parisian Stitch with my numbering.

Fig. 45a. Diagonal Hungarian Ground with my numbering.

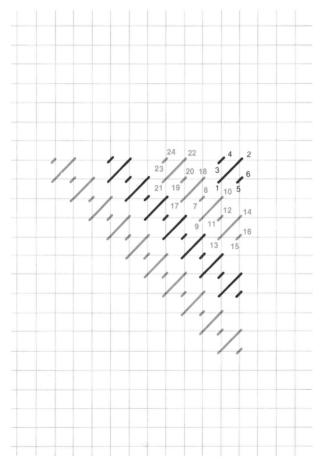

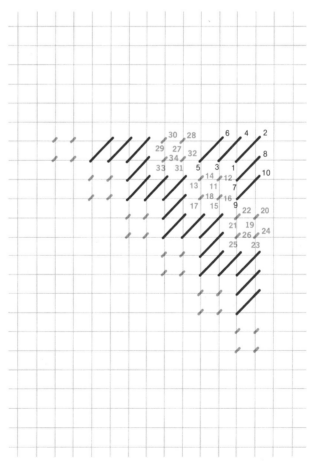

For Your Own Portfolio

Coordinating Pillows by Texture

Staircase Stripes is adaptable for many things other than a telephone book cover. Because of its strong textural nature this design would make an effective accent pillow done in just one color. Just as in relief sculpture, light will be absorbed and reflected by the textured three-dimensional surface and varying light–dark color effects will be brought into play. You will get a certain amount of color variation with just one color because the three-dimensionality of the stitches will cause color variation. Therefore, for any one-color pillow, choose or create a design that combines and uses many different stitches.

Against the one- or two-color pillow, place a gay and busy pattern such as Patchwork I (Color Plates 3 and 5) or Robbing Peter to Pay Paul (Color Plate 18). Or if you wish to make a grouping of three pillows, add a pillow in the Mountain Peaks design (Color Plates 13 and 16). Or use two similar pillows at the ends and a different design in the middle. Relate all three with your color scheme.

One Design as the Starting Point for Another

Staircase Stripes can be easily adapted to other sizes and shapes, creating a different overall effect. To fill out a distinctly oblong shape as shown in Fig. 46*, just keep the design as shown for the left-hand section; then flip it over, in your mind, as if it were drawn on transparent paper and as if it were hinged. Use the result of the 180-degree turn for the right-hand section. In Fig. 46* the left-hand side is filled in and the right-hand side is shown in outline to indicate the reversal. Each box represents 4 vertical and 4 horizontal canvas threads. Each dot represents a Double Leviathan Stitch.

The design can be thought of as a highly stylized butterfly. Keep that idea in mind when choosing your colors. Think of the Double Leviathan lines as the veins and markings on a butterfly's wings; do them in brown and white. Work the background areas in soft strong tones of orange, blue-violet and yellow ochre.[5]

Carry this thought to other nonfigurative designs. I once did a design based on right angles, as shown in Fig. 47*. The sketch reminded me of a waterfall, and I used in it colors that made me think of water—blues, turquoises, and violets.

How to Be Creative with Stitches: The Three Stitch Variables

Many stitches are built by elaborating and changing other stitches. Patterns, textures, and what may seem to be complicated stitches can be easily understood and developed.

A single stitch can be changed in three ways:
1. Change the size of the stitch: That is, change the number of canvas threads it crosses. (See Fig. 48a.)
2. Change the direction of the stitch: That is, change whatever way the stitch points. (See Fig. 48b.)
3. Change the movement of the stitch: That is, groups of stitches can move in a horizontal, vertical, or diagonal direction. A stitch which you see or learn in a horizontal movement can also usually be done in a vertical or diagonal movement. (See Fig. 48c.)

By contrasting the size or length of the stitches used, you can create patterns that clearly show the stitches in vertical and horizontal movements. (See Fig. 48d.) When Fig. 48d is developed into a filling, it becomes what is called the Jacquard Stitch. (See Fig. 48e.)

The three stitch variables then are size, direction, and movement. Any stitch can be modified. Keeping these three variables in mind will help you to understand and achieve textural variation. You can change one, two, or all the variables.

In the fillings of Staircase Stripes, I changed two of the variables—size and movement—and kept one variable constant—direction. The fillings were varied, but were always kept within the boundary of using diagonal stitches, pointing in the same direction.

Color use can be related. In general, when the stitch units forming a filling are without change in size, direction, or movement, you need change of color to

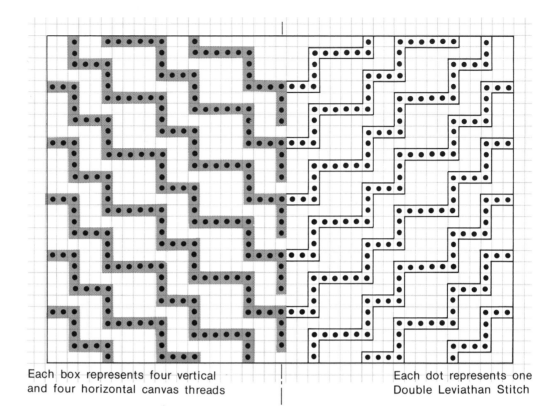

Each box represents four vertical
and four horizontal canvas threads

CENTER

Each dot represents one
Double Leviathan Stitch

Fig. 46*. Stylized butterfly developed from staircase stripes.
Approximate dimensions using No. 12 mono canvas are
11 x 18 inches.

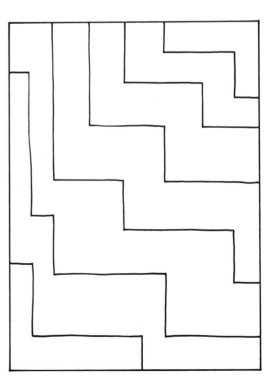

Fig. 47*. Sketch for waterfall design.

bring out texture and patterns. When units are different and there is a change in any or all the variables, the filling can be monochromatic and texture and pattern contrasts can still be achieved.

Feel free to vary stitches. No one has decreed that all stitches must be done the way they once appeared in an embroidery. It is the willingness to change something, the willingness to think of the possibility of change, that makes effective integration of stitches possible.

As you see what the different stitches have in common—or what they don't have in common—you will find them easy to work with and to adjust to your design needs. You will also find it easy to make up unified and meaningful designs from the stitch point of view.

THE THREE STITCH VARIABLES

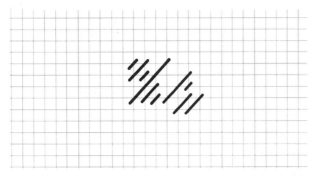

Fig. 48a. Changing the size of the stitch.

Fig. 48b. Changing the direction of the stitch.

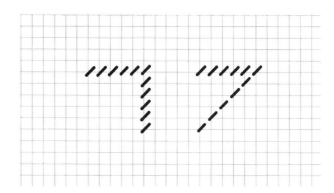

Fig. 48c. Changing the movement of the stitch.

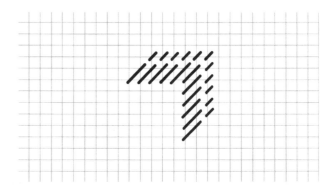

Fig. 48d. Pattern showing vertical and horizontal movement.

Fig. 48e. Jacquard stitch developed from Fig. 48d.

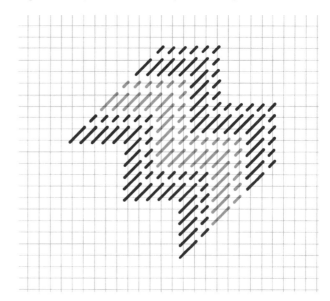

The Visual Unity of a Design

Staircase Stripes is based on contrasting wide striped areas and narrow ones. There is a visual connection between all the wide background areas, so that you feel one whole rectangular shape behind the Double Leviathan Stitches—even though this shape is broken into parts of different colors.

Using fillings or textures all based on diagonal stitches helped to achieve the unity of the background area. Once the background area is seen as one whole shape, you then see more clearly against it, or in contrast to it, the narrow staircase stripes. This makes a more interesting visual statement than a simple repeat pattern of thick and thin staircase stripes.

This brings up a very important point in needlepoint designing. Every time I design a piece of needlepoint I ask myself: "Does this design look as though it came from one bolt of material? Does it look like it could be one piece of fabric? Does this present to my eye one whole unity?"

I want to stress that the question "Does it look as though it could be one piece of fabric" does not mean that the quality or feeling or treatment from part to part must be the same, thereby achieving a dull and uniform design. In fact, contrast is important in the creation of any unity.

Visual unity means that, although there are variety, difference and contrast from part to part, the parts add up to what in your eye becomes unity.

No one element stands out as being foreign to the finished piece. A larger visual concept holds the work together though within a limited and structured framework contrasts and variations abound.

In designing a piece of needlepoint, I keep in mind that I am creating a whole structure. The structure is made up of parts. To give interest, variety and significance, I try to make the parts different and yet related so that they do hold together. You make the parts hold together by choosing your limitations and framework.

You can choose a stitch variable—direction—as in Staircase Stripes, for a textural limitation. The Double Leviathan Stitch which is composed of stitches going in all directions is used as a textural accent. You can choose a color chord, contrast, or scheme for your color limitation. Staircase Stripes is based on blues and greens—analogous or related colors—with a touch of red-violet for accent.

There is a great deal of variety, purely from the stitch point of view, in Staircase Stripes. Although as many as five different stitches are used, the texture as well as the color variation is restrained and kept within bounds, so as to present to the eye a structured unity. I do not feel as if part of this design belonged to something else. To attain consistency and unity through variation and contrast in this design, I followed two of my favorite rules: (1) Say what you mean and mean it, while exercising restraint. (2) Construct a simple outline, making it rich in material and detail.

The unity of any visual statement is important. When designing needlepoint, we should all strive to create a visual unity, keeping in mind that we won't always succeed totally. The trying is the important part!

Ask yourself: Does my eye feel something does not belong? Does my eye feel blocked as it moves from part to part of the design? You will find, I am sure, that you have a good innate sense of visual unity. Just allow your eye to do the work for you; it's probably more reliable than you imagine. And don't forget: we all do see things differently. For instance, you may not see Staircase Stripes at all the way I do!

Plate 18. Robbing Peter to Pay Paul.

Robbing Peter to Pay Paul

Step-by-Step Directions

[*Color Plates 18 and 19*]

MATERIALS:

No. 10 mono canvas

Persian yarn

DIMENSIONS:

17 x 17 inches

168 canvas threads by 168 canvas threads (seam allowance is not included)

STITCHES	ILLUSTRATIONS
Tent Stitch	Figs. 5a, 5b, 5c, 5d, 5e
Double Leviathan Stitch	Figs. 4a, 4b, 4c, 4d, 4e
Scotch Stitch over 5 canvas threads	Fig. 10

In Photo 25, a section corresponding to the oblong pattern shown in Chart 3 is outlined.

Explanation of the Stitch Pattern: How Color Can Change a Stitch Pattern

Robbing Peter to Pay Paul is built on a repetition of one square. This one square, shown in Photo 26, is repeated over and over again, always using the same stitch pattern, but constantly changing the colors.

A Double Leviathan Stitch is in the center of the square. Then 4 Tent Stitch oblongs are added. Each oblong is 5 Tent Stitches by 4 Tent Stitches—20 Tent Stitches in all. By putting a rectangle next to each side of the Double Leviathan Stitch, a cross is formed. (*See* Fig. 49a.)

To fill the cross out to form one large square, a smaller square is put in each corner. Each of these 4 squares is a Scotch Stitch over 5 canvas threads, the diagonal stitches slanting in either of two directions. (*See* Fig. 49b.)

Photo 25. Robbing Peter to Pay Paul.

Color Numbers and Amounts Needed Robbing Peter to Pay Paul

Color	Approximate Amount	Colbert 6	Paterna
Medium yellow-green	4 ounces	91	550
Very light yellow-green	2 ounces	93	580
Deep gold-yellow	2½ ounces	55	440
Burnt orange	5½ ounces	30	424
Medium olive green	4 ounces	27	553
Green earth	2½ ounces	104	527
Forest green	4 ounces	108	528
Very deep rust	4 ounces	61	210
Deep rust	1 ounce	62	245
Brownish black	1½ ounces	136	105
White	5½ ounces	174	005

Photo 26. One square of Robbing Peter to Pay Paul.

If color were used to bring out the pattern formed with the stitches, an image that looks like the one you see in Fig. 49c would result: one large square made up of a cross and 4 squares, one in each corner.

Instead, I can keep this stitch pattern, but by using color to break it, I obtain the image shown in Fig. 49d: one large square with an uneven-sided octagon imposed on top of it. Each of the 4 Scotch Stitch squares is divided approximately in half, producing 2 triangles in each Scotch Stitch square. In Fig. 49e you can see that it is impossible to divide a Scotch Stitch square into two equal triangles. This is because there is always an uneven number of diagonal stitches in a Scotch Stitch.

Plate 19. Detail of Robbing Peter to Pay Paul.

The uneven-sided octagon is created by making each of the triangles (4 diagonal stitches) that join the Tent Stitch oblongs the same color as the Tent Stitching. (*See* Fig. 49d.) The Double Leviathan Stitch can be the same or another color, as you wish. In this design, in every case, I have made the Double Leviathan center of each square a different color than the octagon.

It is interesting to see what happens visually when several of the squares are put together. Diamond shapes, each composed of four triangles, appear between the octagons. (*See* Color Plate **19**.)

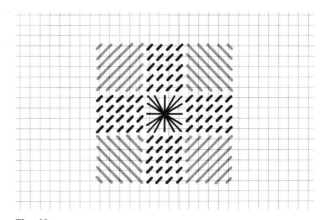

Fig. 49c.

ANALYSIS OF ONE SQUARE OF ROBBING PETER TO PAY PAUL

Fig. 49a.

Fig. 49d.

Fig. 49b.

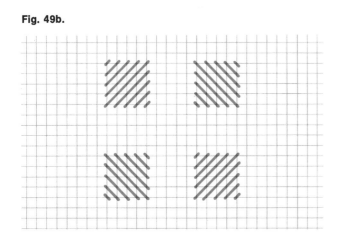

Fig. 49e.

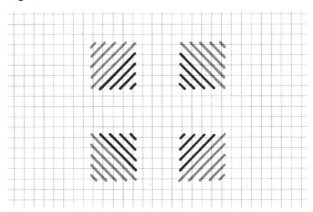

Step 1

Work from Chart 3, to stitch the first 12 squares on your canvas. Use 3-ply yarn throughout.

■ The stitch pattern for each square is included in the chart so that you will remember which stitches to use for each color. A section that corresponds to Chart 3 is shown in outline in Photo 25.

■ Start in the upper left-hand corner with the first white triangle of the first Scotch Stitch square. There will be 5 diagonal stitches in this triangle.

■ Then do the burnt-orange triangle completing the first Scotch Stitch square. There will be 4 diagonal stitches in this triangle.

■ Continue with the burnt-orange Tent Stitching, making all the necessary stitch and color changes until you have completed the first square of the oblong pattern. The center of this first square is a brownish-black Double Leviathan Stitch.

■ Do all the remaining 11 squares in the same fashion.

■ You may find it helpful when doing this design to keep several needles going threaded with the various colors.

Step 2

Fill out the rest of the pillow by repeating the oblong which is now set up on your canvas. Work from the canvas itself, or from the chart, as you prefer. Repeat the oblong three more times across the pillow and two more times down the pillow. *Turn the oblong upside down every time you repeat it.* This is just a trick to make the design appear as if no pattern were used.

■ Notice that you can make a small, medium, or large pillow, depending upon how often you repeat the oblong, and how much of it you choose to repeat.

Step 3

Add 4 rows of Tent Stitching all around the design in the appropriate colors, for the upholsterer's seam allowance.

This design requires a great deal of wool (1) because it is a large pillow and (2) because of the skipping around that you must do with the colors. Use whatever leftovers you have to invent your own design to go with Robbing Peter to Pay Paul.

For Your Own Portfolio

Color is used in Robbing Peter to Pay Paul (Color Plate 18) to create a pattern that appears to have constant variation, a pattern with no rhyme or reason. In fact, the main idea of Robbing Peter to Pay Paul is breaking the pattern. It is one of my favorite designs, because all the visual variety is obtained with simple means.

Eleven colors are used. Two of the colors are black and white. The others move in chroma quality from very deep rust, or reddish orange, to burnt orange, yellow, yellow-green, and green. I think of these colors as fall colors.

The colors also progress from the very deepest, brownish black, to the deep rust and deep green, through medium-value shades, such as the green earth and the burnt orange, all the way up through the very light yellow-green to finally the lightest color, white.

These colors vary, and yet are related in hue or chroma. There is also a wide variation in lightness and darkness among the 11 colors. This is a design that can take a great deal of color variation because there are so many small areas to fill in.

If you wish to make your own color version of Robbing Peter to Pay Paul, just choose a group of colors that you like. Make sure you have a wide range of light–dark variation, and then have fun doing each square as you like, following your own instinct. Incidentally, this is a good design to work if you wish to use leftover colors from other projects; it's also a good choice if you want to experiment with color effects. Robbing Peter to Pay Paul can also be done on No. 12 mono canvas with 2-ply Persian yarn. You can use the same canvas thread count, but the dimensions in inches of the pillow will be smaller.

I designed Robbing Peter to Pay Paul to coordinate with a color version of Mountain Peaks. Later, a client who had made Robbing Peter to Pay Paul to put on a lemon yellow floral-pattern sofa wanted to make another pillow to go with it. She saw and liked a small experimental texture in my studio, and so I designed Mysterious Islands (Color Plate 28). The two pillows are a handsome combination.

Chart 3 Color Key for
Robbing Peter to Pay Paul
W — White
BO — Burnt orange
BB — Brownish black
FG — Forest green
MYG — Medium yellow-green
DR — Deep rust
VDR — Very deep rust
MOG — Medium olive green
GE — Green earth
DGY — Deep gold-yellow
VLYG — Very light yellow-green

On-the-Bias Designs

Technique

When needlepoint canvas is cut to create the rectangular shape of the design it is usually cut on the straight, that is, at right angles or parallel to the selvages. To cut on the straight means to cut parallel to the canvas threads. (*See* Photo 27.)

Needlepoint canvas can also be cut on the bias. To cut on the bias, cut at a 45-degree angle or diagonal to the intersecting threads of the canvas. (*See* Photo 28.)

To understand fully what happens to stitches when the bias cut is used, I suggest that you take a piece of practice canvas and follow along with me.

1. Keep the selvage to your left and right. Make a grid of Double Leviathan Stitches as shown in Fig. 50. Fill in the center square with Tent Stitching. Imagine how the design would look if you cut the canvas on the straight: just as it faces you now—the Double Leviathan Stitches forming a rectangular grid.

2. Now cut the canvas on the bias or on the diagonal, as shown by the broken lines in Fig. 50.

3. After you have cut the canvas, turn it to a horizontal position, so it looks like Fig. 51.

▪ The cutting lines will now be at top and bottom in a horizontal position. The selvages now go in a diagonal direction, not a vertical direction.

▪ Each Double Leviathan Stitch looks like a diamond, not a square. All the Double Leviathan Stitches, instead of forming a grid as they do in Fig. 50, now form a diamond shape.

▪ The canvas threads no longer make a checkerboard of horizontal and vertical threads facing you, as they do in Fig. 50. Now, as in Fig. 51, the canvas threads go in diagonal directions, but of course, still at right angles to each other.

▪ The Tent Stitches that you did in the square in Fig. 50 now look like tiny Brick Stitches inside of the diamond in Fig. 51.

Photo 27. Needlepoint canvas cut on the straight.

Photo 28. Needlepoint canvas cut on the bias.

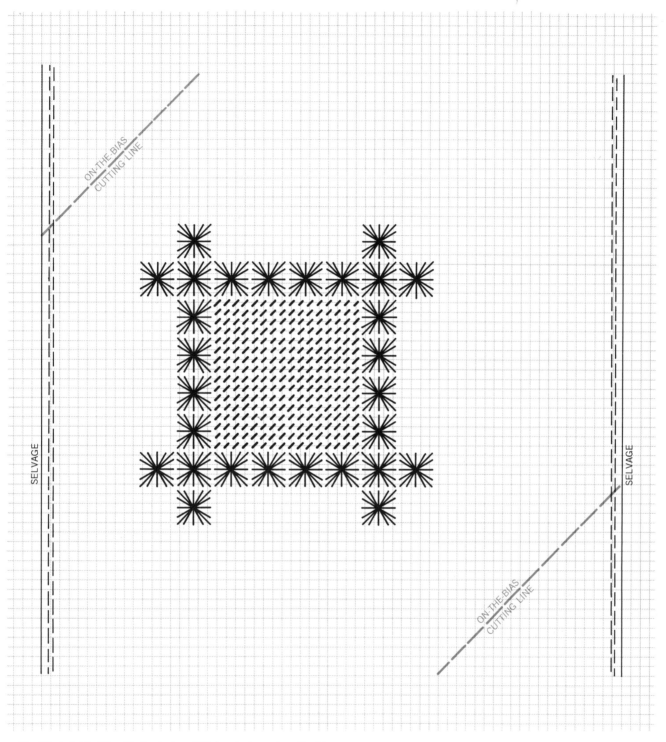

Fig. 50. A Grid of Double Leviathan Stitches to be cut on the bias.

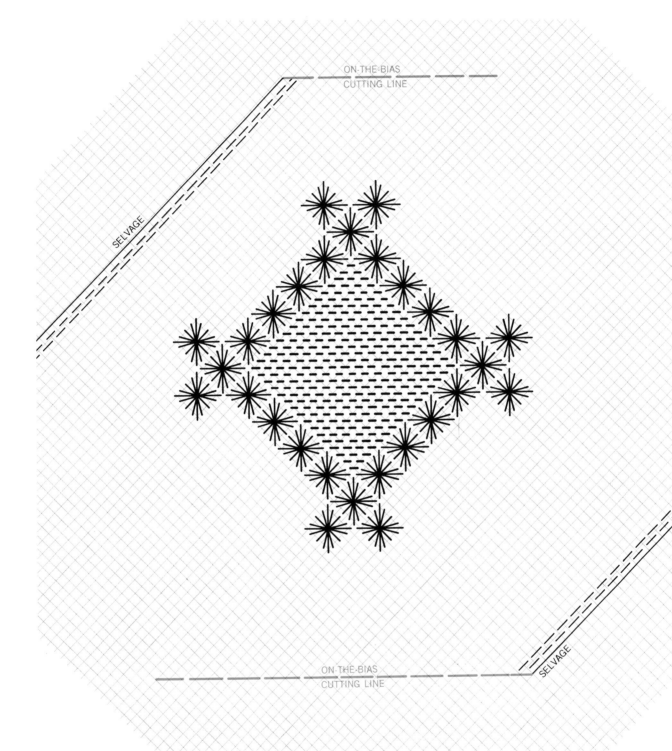

Fig. 51. After grid of Fig. 50 is cut on the bias, turn it to a horizontal position.

How to Cut and Work On-the-Bias Designs

1. Keep the selvages to the left and right. Cutting diagonally, or on the bias, cut out of the canvas the shape and dimensions you desire.

Before I cut on the bias, I stitch with long basting stitches the diagonal line close to which I will cut. This makes it easier to get a straight diagonal edge. (*See* Photo 29.) I add a margin of at least 2 inches around the dimensions of the design. In other words, I add at least 4 inches and sometimes 6 inches to the dimensions of the design to determine the size of the canvas I will cut out.

2. After you have cut out the shape, bind the diagonal or bias raw edges. (*See* Photo 30.)

3. Keep the selvages to the left and right, and work the stitches in the usual fashion. Photo 30 shows how to hold the canvas when working. Notice that the canvas threads make a grid of horizontal and vertical threads facing you.

4. If you wish to see how your finished design will look, turn the diagonal edge that you cut and bound to a horizontal position. (*See* Photo 31.) Now the canvas threads go in diagonal directions, but still at right angles to each other.

5. Remember that just as in dressmaking, when you cut a square or rectangular shape on the bias, you will need slightly more yardage of material. As a result, on-the-bias belts are costlier than on-the-straight belts. The extra amount that you will need depends on the dimensions of your piece.

For example, the finished dimensions of the Harlequin Studded Belt (Photo 32, page 77) are 28 inches long by 3½ inches wide. A working piece of canvas 32 inches long and 7½ inches wide (providing a 2-inch margin all around the dimensions of the belt) is needed. To obtain this it can be cut out of a piece of canvas 28 inches long and 31 inches wide. Out of a piece of canvas 1 yard long and 1 yard wide, you can get several on-the-bias belts. Therefore, it is wise to keep a yard or two of canvas on hand only for on-the-bias designs. A large triangular leftover could be used for a needlepoint kerchief. And, of course, you can always cut on-the-straight squares and rectangles out

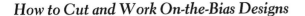

31 inches wide

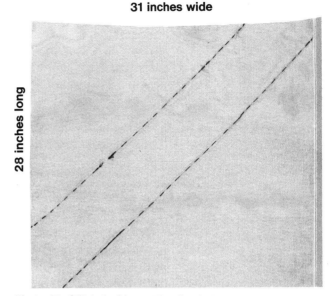

28 inches long

Photo 29. Stitch the bias cutting line before you cut.

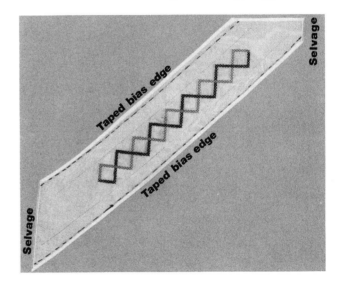

Photo 30. Canvas shape with bias edges bound with tape. Armature of Harlequin Studded Belt is shown. How to hold the canvas when working.

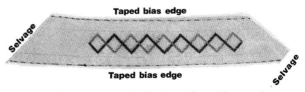

Photo 31. Photo 30 turned to horizontal position so that you can visualize how finished belt will appear.

of any leftover pieces. Several on-the-straight belts are shown further on. (*See* Color Plates **37** and **45**, Photo **44**.)

Cutting and using canvas on the bias enables you to:
1. Use a square stitch as a diamond shape.
2. Use a diagonal stitch as a vertical or horizontal stitch.
3. Use a vertical or horizontal stitch as a diagonal stitch.

In other words, the technique of cutting and using canvas on the bias enables you to double the number of visual effects obtainable with your stitch repertoire.

Once you get used to working on the bias, you will find it easy to visualize how a stitch or pattern will look used that way. I usually look at the stitch diagram and turn my head at a 45-degree angle to see how it will appear. You could also just turn the diagram or the book in which the illustration is found.

Belts cut on the bias fit better than those cut on the straight. You may find as you are working on-the-bias designs that the canvas seems to pull out of shape. Do not worry about this; blocking the piece will easily bring it back into shape.

All the on-the-bias designs shown are in belt form. They can easily be adapted for on-the-bias pillows. Recently, I designed a set of dining-room chair seats on the bias. If you do an on-the-bias pillow, I suggest that you size the wrong side of the blocked canvas before mounting, to insure that it holds its shape.[6] This is not necessary for a belt because the leather mounting will make the belt hold its shape.

Fig. 52 shows the on-the-bias stitch pattern used for Byzantine Jewels, No. 3 (Color Plates **20** and **21**). The broken lines indicate the bias cutting line. The Double Leviathan Stitch, Byzantine Stitch over 2 canvas threads, and Tent Stitch are used on No. 12 mono canvas with 2-ply Persian yarn. Keep repeating the pattern until the length of the belt is filled out. This belt was designed to be worn with a navy sweater and pants outfit. I tried to suggest around-the-waist movement by constantly changing the colors.

Fig. 53* shows the on-the-bias stitch pattern used for Byzantine Jewels, No. 1 (Color Plate **22**). The broken lines indicate the bias cutting line. The Double Leviathan Stitch and the Tent Stitch are used on No. 12 mono canvas with 2-ply Persian yarn. Keep repeating the pattern until the length of the belt is filled out. This design was widened and used for a matching eyeglass case.

You can change an on-the-bias design so that it can be used on the straight. Fig. 54* shows a design for a pillow developed from the belt design shown in Fig. 53*. The same stitch pattern is used. The diagonal bands are repeated and alternated to fill out the canvas to make a square shape. For this design, the canvas should be cut on the straight and kept on the straight when mounted. You can, if you wish, apply this same idea to other on-the-bias stitch patterns. However, this is *not* the same as making Fig. 53* into an on-the-bias pillow.

Fig. 54* works nicely on No. 3 rug canvas with rug wool. Instead of using the Tent Stitch as indicated in this illustration, use the Cross Stitch, which works well on No. 3 rug canvas.

Plate 20. Byzantine Jewels, No. 3.

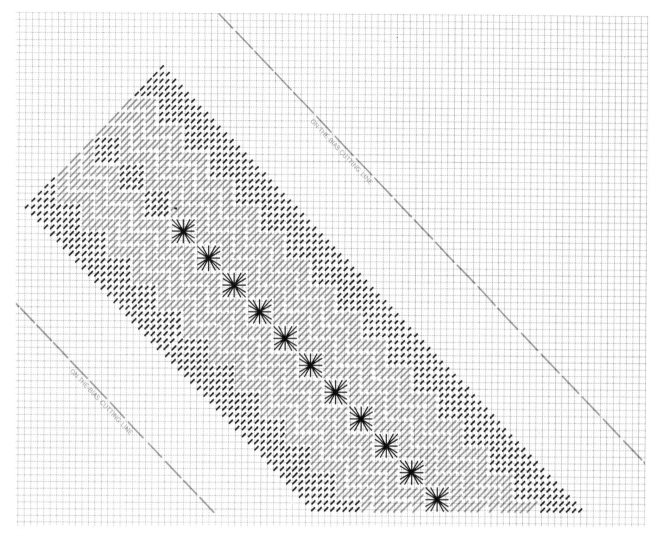

Fig. 52*. On-the-bias stitch pattern for Byzantine Jewels, No. 3.

Plate 21. Detail of Byzantine Jewels, No. 3.

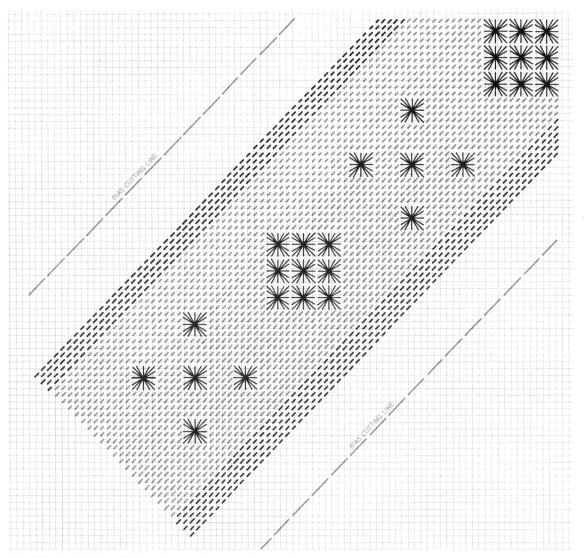

Fig. 53*. On-the-bias stitch pattern for Byzantine Jewels, No. 1.

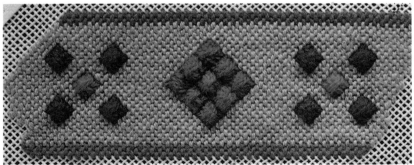

Plate 22. Study for Byzantine Jewels, No. 1.

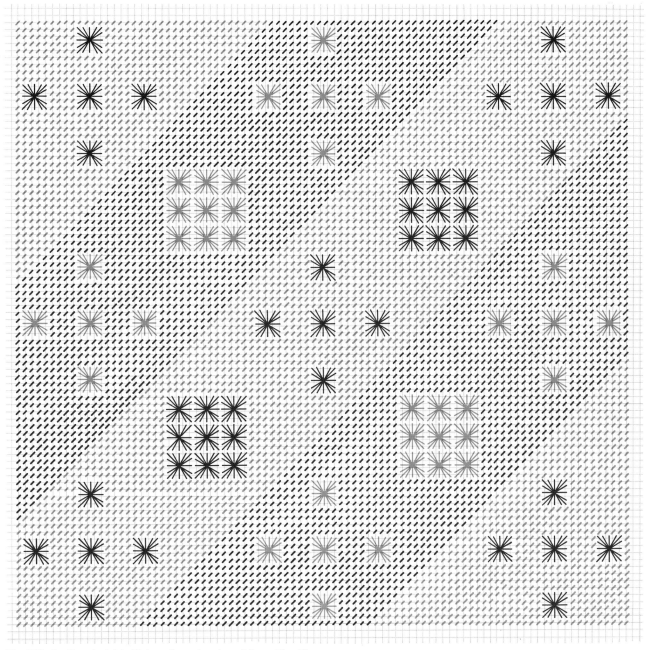

Fig. 54*. On-the-straight stitch pattern developed from Fig. 53.

Plate 23. Detail of Harlequin Studded Belt.

Harlequin Studded Belt
[On-the-Bias Design]

Step-by-Step Directions

[*Color Plate 23*]

MATERIALS:

No. 12 mono canvas

Persian yarn

DIMENSIONS:

28 x 3½ inches (finished needlepoint)

32 x 7½ inches (working piece of canvas cut on the bias)

STITCHES	ILLUSTRATIONS
Double Leviathan Stitch	Figs. 4a, 4b, 4c, 4d, 4e
Tent Stitch	Figs. 5a, 5b, 5c, 5d, 5e
Jacquard Stitch	Fig. 56

The belt shown in Photo 32 is lined with leather. The needlepoint for this type of belt should be worked approximately to correct full waist size. Read the background information for on-the-bias designs on pages 71–72.

Fig. 55* shows the on-the-bias stitch pattern for the Harlequin Studded Belt.

In Fig. 55*, the broken lines indicate the bias cutting line. The arrow points to the Double Leviathan Stitch that should be started at the center back of the belt. Repeat the pattern as shown in the illustration, filling out each side of the belt and working from the center back. In this way you will be able to end off both ends of the belt so that they match each other. The belt shown in Photo 32 has a red-violet diamond

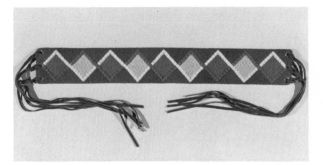

Photo 32. Harlequin Studded Belt.

in the center and at each end, with green and red-violet diamonds alternating between them.

Keep in mind that you can change the number of Double Leviathan Stitches in the framework and thus make this design wider or narrower.

Color Numbers and Amounts Needed
Harlequin Studded Belt

Color	Approximate Amount	Colbert 6	Paterna
Light turquoise	1 ounce	124	748
Deep blue-green	1 ounce	147	718
Light medium warm green	1½ ounces	113	574
Very deep royal blue	1½ ounces	80	721
Deep red-violet	1½ ounces	86	821
Deep olive .green	1½ ounces	26	540

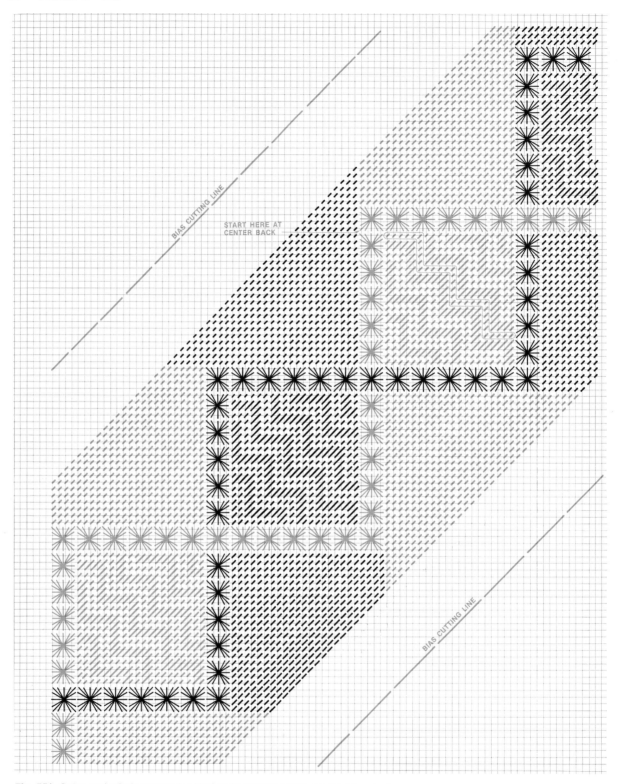

Fig. 55*. Color and stitch pattern for Harlequin Studded belt: on-the-bias design.

Step 1

Keep the selvages of the canvas to the left and right.
■ Baste on the canvas the bias cutting line for the dimensions of the working piece of canvas. Be sure to make any necessary adjustments for correct waist size.
■ Cutting diagonally or on the bias, cut the canvas to the dimensions for the working piece—which you have just marked with basting thread. (*See* Photo 29, page 71.) Refer again if necessary to the details of on-the-bias cutting.

Step 2

Bind the raw edges of the canvas. If you have cut off the selvage edges of the canvas, mark the appropriate taped edges with the word "Selvage" so that you know where they are. (*See* Photo 30, page 71.)

Step 3

Hold the canvas so that the selvage edges are to your left and right. The canvas threads should make a grid of horizontal and vertical threads facing you.
■ Set up the framework of the design by counting out and stitching the armature of each Double Leviathan Stitch. Use 2-ply yarn.
■ Start the first Double Leviathan Stitch at the center back of the belt as indicated by the arrow in Fig. 55*.
■ Refer to Photo 30.

Step 4

Go back and complete each Double Leviathan Stitch. Use 2-ply yarn.

Color key to stitches in Fig. 55

black Double Leviathan Stitches = deep blue-green
red Double Leviathan Stitches = light turquoise
black Jacquard Stitches = light medium warm green
red Jacquard Stitches = deep red-violet
black Tent Stitches = very deep royal blue
red Tent Stitches = deep olive green

Step 5

■ Fill the areas inside the Double Leviathan Stitches with the Jacquard Stitch (Figs. 55* and 56). Fig. 56 shows the Jacquard Stitch in black with the red stitches indicating the fudging stitches that are necessary to square off the filling.
■ The Jacquard Stitch is composed of Diagonal Stitches over 2 canvas threads and Tent Stitches. Use 3-ply yarn for the Diagonal Stitches and 2-ply yarn for the Tent Stitches. Scoop the needle.
■ When working from Fig. 55* start the Jacquard Stitch filling with the row of Tent Stitching that is outlined.

Step 6

Do the remainder of the belt with Tent Stitching. Be sure to add 3 rows of Tent Stitching in the appropriate colors for the mounter's seam allowance.

Step 7

Turn the bound bias edges of the belt to a horizontal position so that you can see how the finished belt appears.

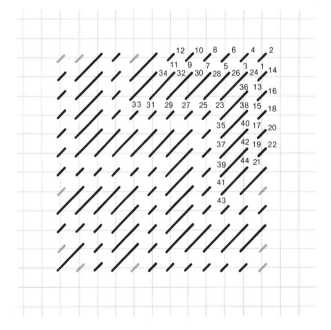

Fig. 56. Jacquard Stitch.

Plate 24. Lady's Tennis Racquet Cover.

Lady's Tennis Racquet Cover

Step-by-Step Directions

[*Color Plate 24*]

MATERIALS:

    No. 12 mono canvas
    Persian yarn
    Tapestry wool

STITCHES	ILLUSTRATIONS
Tent Stitch	Figs. 5a, 5b, 5c, 5d, 5e
Twisted Satin Stitch	Fig. 57, 57a
Woven Wheel Stitch	Fig. 58, 58a
Whipped Double Running Stitch	Fig. 59
French Knots	Fig. 60
Back Stitch	Fig. 61
Long and Short Stitch	Fig. 62
Chain Stitch	Fig. 63
Broad Chain with Back Stitch	Fig. 64

This tennis racquet cover was designed for a Head Master aluminum racquet. The exact pattern needed for a tennis racquet cover depends upon the make and model of the racquet. I suggest that you obtain a paper pattern, before starting the design, from the individual or firm who will do the mounting. If you write to Modern Needlepoint Mounting Company, 11 West 32 Street, New York, New York 10001, specifying the make and model of your racquet, they will send you a paper pattern for a slight charge. Be sure to mention whether the racquet is wood or metal.

If you do not wish to make a tennis racquet cover, you can still do this design by adapting it for a Portrait Wall Hanging.

Work from Color Plate **24**. (The male partner for this design is shown in Photo 36, page 111.)

Step 1

Copy the head using the color plate as a model.
- Draw on the canvas with a light-gray permanent marking pen or with permanent paint.
- Try to make the features and curls firm, strong, and simple. Copy from my design to the best of your ability. If yours does not look exactly like mine, do not worry. You will be putting your own personality into your piece.

Step 2

Surround the eyes, eyelashes, eyebrows, nose, mouth, curls, and rouge spots with 1 row of Tent Stitching (Fig. 5a), using the background color. Use 2-ply Persian yarn.

Color Numbers and Amounts Needed
Lady's Tennis Racquet Cover

Color	Approximate Amount	Colbert 6	Paterna
Persian Yarn			
Sherbet pink (background)	8 ounces	178	865
White	¼ ounce	174	005
Cool pink	¼ ounce	168	839
Deep red-violet	½ ounce	86	821
Maroon	¼ ounce	173	236
Black	1 ounce	137	050

Tapestry Wool		Laine Colbert au Bon Pasteur
Warm pink	2 skeins	Rose de France—3
Royal blue	1 skein	Bleu de nuit—4
Turquoise	1 skein	Bleu de mer—5
Black	1 skein	Noir

Step 3

Work the eyes.

Eyeballs: Worked with Tent Stitch in 2-ply white Persian yarn.

Pupils: Worked with Twisted Satin Stitch (Figs. 57 and 57a) in black tapestry wool.

Iris: Use Woven Wheel Stitch (Figs. 58 and 58a) and tapestry wool in royal blue, turquoise and black.

■ Set up odd number of spokes with royal blue tapestry wool. *Do not pull spokes tight. It is better to leave them loose.*

■ Weave around black pupil under and over spokes with royal blue tapestry wool, then turquoise, then black, as shown in the color plate.

Outline each eye with Whipped Double Running Stitch (Fig. 59), using black tapestry wool.

Eyelashes: Use French Knots (Fig. 60) in black tapestry wool.

Step 4

Work the rouge spots with the Woven Wheel Stitch (Figs. 58 and 58a). Use warm pink tapestry wool; 3-ply Persian yarn in cool pink and red-violet.

■ Set up an odd number of spokes with warm pink tapestry wool. You may find that one center hole gets too filled with wool and that you have to use a second hole. *Do not pull spokes too tight. It is better to leave them loose.*

■ Weave around the spokes with the three shades of pink as shown in the color plate: (1) cool pink, (2) red violet, and (3) warm pink.

■ You can add more spokes out near the circumference, between the threads already laid if the distance between the spokes gets too long or sloppy-looking.[7]

■ You may find it necessary to do some Tent Stitching with the background color underneath the outer edges of the rouge spots.

Fig. 57. Twisted Satin Stitch.

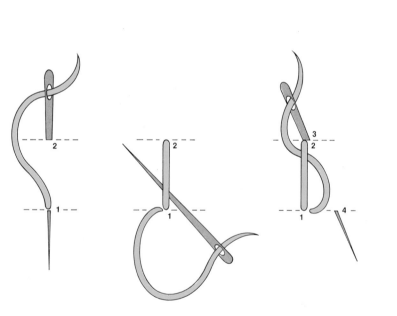

Fig. 57a. The Twisted Satin Stitch on needlepoint canvas.

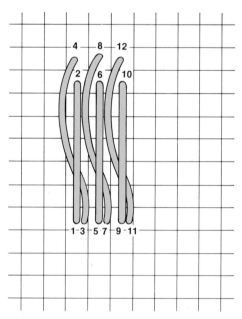

When following your drawing of the pupil, you can judge where to put the needle in at 2 by thinking ahead where you will put it in at 4.

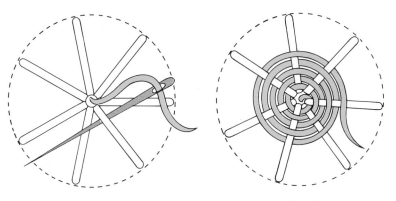

Step 1   Step 2

Fig. 58. Woven Wheel Stitch or Woven Spider Web.

Fig. 59. Whipped Double Running Stitch.

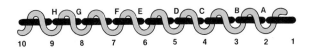

1. First do the stitches indicated by the numbers.

2. Then do the stitches indicated by the letters.

3. The red line shows, in exaggerated form, the whipping thread. Whip over each Running Stitch without entering material or canvas.

4. When working Double Running Stitch on canvas, make stitches as large or as small as you judge necessary to follow the line.

Fig. 58a. The Woven Wheel Stitch (Woven Spider Web) on needlepoint canvas.

Fig. 60. French Knot.

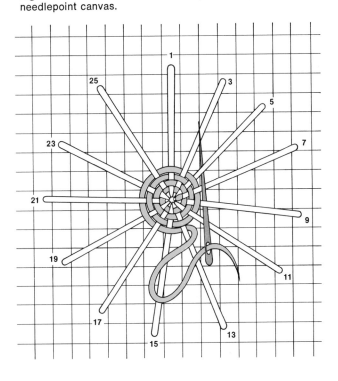

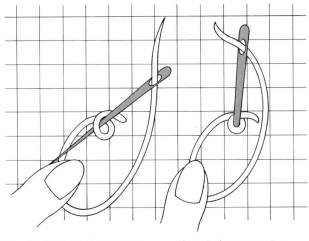

Step 1. Hold the thread down with your left thumb. Wrap the thread around the needle once.

Step 2. Insert needle into next hole.

Step 5

Work the lips.

Outline the lips in Back Stitching (Fig. 61). Use 3-ply maroon Persian yarn.

Fill in the lips in Long and Short Stitching (Fig. 62), Use 2-ply red-violet Persian yarn.

■ Do the Long and Short Stitch in a free manner, changing the direction of the stitches from top to bottom lips, as in the color plate.

Step 6

Work the nose in Chain Stitching (Fig. 63). Use 3-ply black Persian yarn.

Step 7

Work the curls.

Do the outer ends of the curls at the edge of the tennis racquet cover.

■ Use Tent Stitching in 2-ply black Persian yarn. You are doing this to make a smooth area at the edge of the cover for mounting.

Do the remaining areas of the curls. Use the Broad Chain with Back Stitch (Fig. 64) in 3-ply black Persian yarn.

Step 8

Fill in the background with Tent Stitching (Fig. 5b). Use 2-ply sherbet pink Persian yarn.

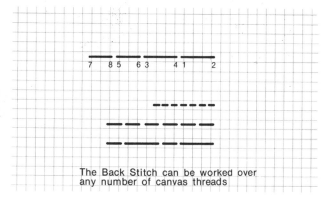

The Back Stitch can be worked over any number of canvas threads

Fig. 61. The Back Stitch.

Fig. 62. Long and Short Stitch (Tapestry Shading Stitch).

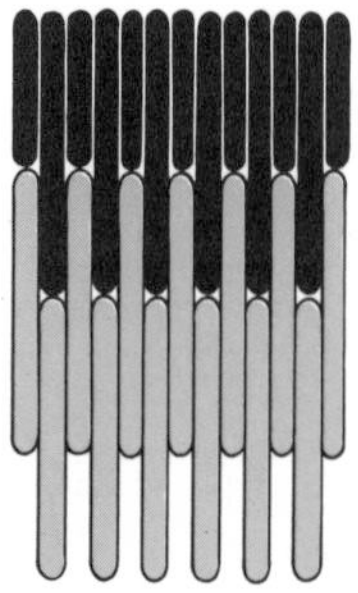

The Long and Short Stitch is a form of Satin Stitch in which the stitches are of varying lengths. It is a good stitch to use when filling an irregular shape such as the mouth on the Lady's Tennis Racquet Cover. You can be very flexible with this stitch.

Fig. 63. Chain Stitch.

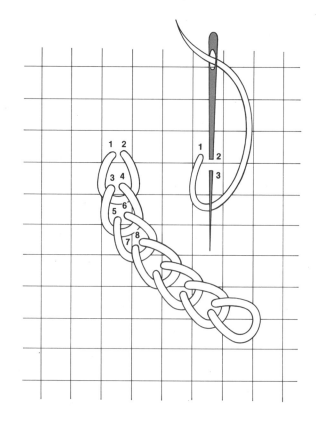

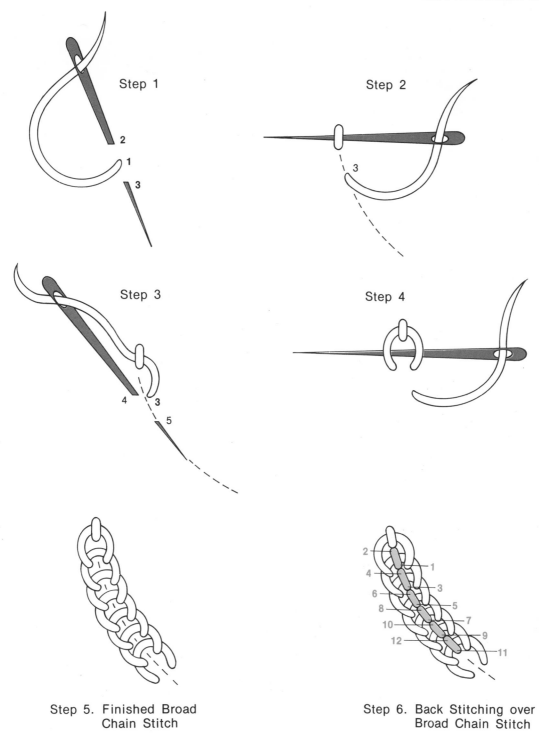

Step 1

Step 2

Step 3

Step 4

Step 5. Finished Broad
Chain Stitch

Step 6. Back Stitching over
Broad Chain Stitch

Dotted line indicates line you are following

Fig. 64. Broad Chain with Back Stitch.

Plate 25. Detail of Tree in Adam and Eve Wall Hanging.

Woven and Sculptural Textures and Designs: An Overview of Experimental Techniques

I started thinking about the possibility of using weaving and embroidery techniques on needlepoint canvas because of my desire to experiment with colors.

Generally in needlepoint designs—as in most paintings—one puts colors side by side, and that predicates to a great extent the color effects that can be achieved.

In working with needlepoint stitches other than the Tent Stitch, I realized that many stitches are built up in layers: the Double Leviathan Stitch (Fig. 65a), the Double Straight Cross Stitch (Fig. 65b), the Renaissance Stitch (Fig. 65c), the Rice Stitch (Fig. 65d), and even the simple Cross Stitch (Fig. 65e).

If a stitch is constructed in two or more layers, it is possible to do the first layer in one color and one type of thread, and the second layer in another color or another type of thread. This will produce higher and lower levels as well as an over–under or layered effect similar to a woven surface. It is particularly by using layered stitches that one develops three-dimensional designs in needlepoint.

MANY NEEDLEPOINT STITCHES ARE DONE IN LAYERS.

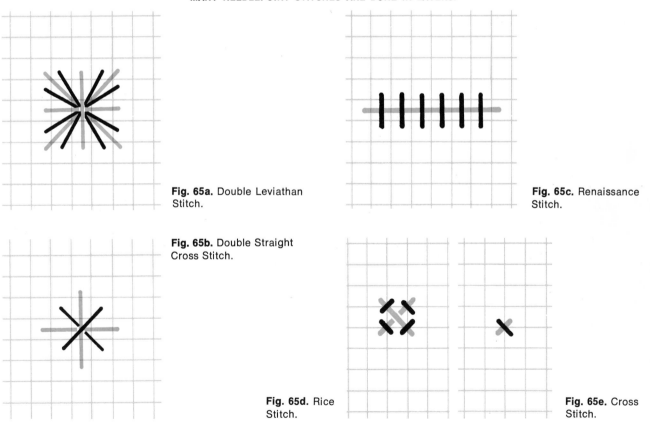

Fig. 65a. Double Leviathan Stitch.

Fig. 65b. Double Straight Cross Stitch.

Fig. 65c. Renaissance Stitch.

Fig. 65d. Rice Stitch.

Fig. 65e. Cross Stitch.

Plate 26. Cat Pillow.

THE CAT PILLOW

[*Color Plates 26 and 27*]

One of the first designs in which I used colors in layers was the Cat Pillow. This pillow is done on No. 5 double-mesh rug canvas (5/10) with rug wool, Persian yarn and French silk. (I use Paternayan Pat-Rug yarn and Soie d'Alger silk.) In the head, tail and a small section of the body, the canvas is used 10 holes to the inch; in the other parts of the design, the canvas is used 5 holes to the inch.

There are three layers of stitching in the head and tail. First, I used Tramé or understitching (*see* pages 90–91) in 1-ply Persian yarn. Then Tent-Stitching over the Tramé, again in 1-ply Persian yarn, I worked out the eventual arrangement of my colors. Next I Tent-Stitched over that with double-weight French silk. Embroidery cotton is a very good substitute for the silk; it is much cheaper and it is easier to use.

Although there are three layers of stitching in the cat's head and tail, the finished areas are not too bulky and the stitching fits the canvas just right. The appropriate weights for each layer are:

Layer 1: Tramé in 1-ply Persian yarn
Layer 2: Tent Stitching in 1-ply Persian yarn
Layer 3: Tent Stitching in 14-ply French silk

The background of the Cat Pillow (Color Plate 27) is built on the idea of using different colors in layers. In this case, the colors in the first layer play a most important role.

I particularly wanted to use rug wool in the background of the pillow to achieve a contrast of scale: bulkiness contrasted with the fineness of the head and tail. Also, I wanted to use up-and-down stitches in the background, to contrast with the predominantly diagonal stitches of the head, tail, and body.

I decided to try to use the Brick Stitch (Fig. 66) on the rug canvas. When I first tried to do the Brick Stitch on the double-mesh canvas, 5 holes to the inch,

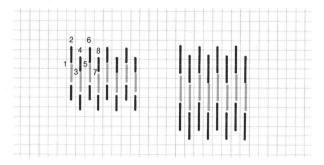

Fig. 66. Brick Stitch. Various sizes.

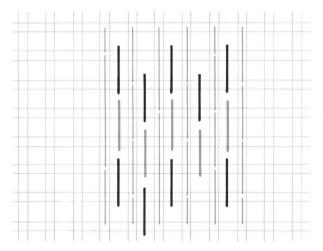

Fig. 67*. Brick Stitch on double-mesh rug canvas with Tramé in vertical narrow channels.

the narrow vertical channels of canvas showed through.

Covering the narrow vertical channels first with Tramé in long Back Stitches in the silk solved that problem. I found the number of ply silk that was necessary to keep the canvas from showing through. Then all I had to do was to fill in the Brick Stitches with the rug wool in the wide channels. (See Fig. 67*.)

A whole pillow could be done beautifully in the background texture that is used for the cat.

The Importance of Tramé in Developing Needlepoint Textures

There is an important needlepoint technique with which you are probably familiar: Tramé.

As traditionally defined, Tramé is an "underlay of colored yarn thread placed over the horizontal meshes that are close together in double-thread canvas."[8] "[Tramé] is an old European method of padding stitches. It is never used by itself, but as a foundation for other stitches."[9]

I use Tramé in vertical as well as horizontal directions, on single-thread or mono canvas, as well as on double-thread or Penelope canvas. Of course, the length of the Tramé stitches varies, depending upon the situation. And at times, I do use Tramé by itself. (See Figs. 68a and 68b.)

In some fine traditional European needlepoint canvases that are professionally designed, Tramé is used rather than paint to indicate where what colors should be filled in. Also, Sylvia Sidney, in the *Sylvia Sidney Needlepoint Book*, mentions that Tramé can be used as "underpainting"[10]—an excellent idea.

In embroidery, Tramé would be considered and referred to as Laid Work.[11] Laid Work is usually tied down or couched by various types of stitches. You could consider the Cross Stitch Tramé (Fig. 69) as Laid Work tied down or couched by Cross Stitches.

Many needlepoint stitches use Tramé in their construction. In addition to the Cross Stitch Tramé, there is the Tent Stitch Tramé (Fig. 70) and the Renaissance Stitch (Fig. 73, page 97). The Cross Stitch armature of the Double Leviathan Stitch can also be thought of as Tramé.

An embroidery stitch that I have adapted for use on needlepoint canvas and which involves Laid Work, and therefore Tramé in needlepoint, is the Recent Burden Stitch (Fig. 71). The Recent Burden Stitch is simply a large Brick Stitch over Tramé.[12] The use of Tramé enables one to build a stitch in layers as well as to pad or raise a stitch. The Recent Burden Stitch is used extensively in the Creation Panels (Photos 46, 47, and 48, page 123).

By allowing Tramé—the substructure—to be seen I have expanded the concept and use of Tramé. Instead of thinking of Tramé as something that should be hidden, I have exposed it.

By doing this, I have finally been able to achieve in needlepoint something I had always wanted to do in painting: I found a technique for using colors in layers—actually having physical layers of color. Now I can obtain color effects based on colors lying underneath or on top of each other, instead of only side by side. Now I am able to use color in a three-dimensional way.

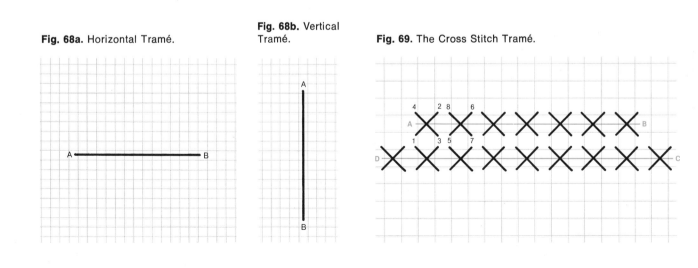

Fig. 68a. Horizontal Tramé.

Fig. 68b. Vertical Tramé.

Fig. 69. The Cross Stitch Tramé.

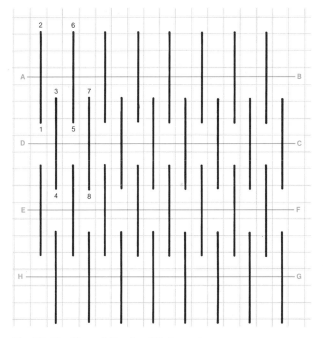

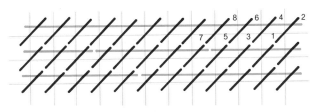

Fig. 70. The Tent Stitch Tramé.

Fig. 71. The Recent Burden Stitch.

Plate 27. Detail of Cat Pillow.

Plate 28. Mysterious Islands.

MYSTERIOUS ISLANDS

[*Color Plate 28*]

Mysterious Islands is based on the effect of two layers of color as well as on a traditional weaving concept: layers of yarn at right angles to each other.

The design is done on the same type of canvas as the Cat Pillow—No. 5 double-mesh canvas (5/10). Rug wool is used. This design is most easily done with a frame, either a hand or floor type. You could also stretch the canvas on canvas stretchers. I prefer to use either a floor frame or canvas stretchers because, using them, I can see my whole design developing, and therefore am able to make designing decisions as I go along.

The first step is to lay the warp or, in needlepoint terms, lay the Tramé. Long pieces of rug wool are laid from the top edge of the design to the bottom edge as shown in Fig. 72. Each piece of rug wool covers a wide vertical channel of the double-mesh canvas, leaving the narrow channels mostly uncovered. You can leave the ends of the wool hanging at either end of the canvas to be used as part of a fringe, or you can finish them off now or later.

The next step is to cross the warp or Tramé, at right angles, with Running Stitches as shown in Fig. 72. Start each horizontal row by positioning the piece of rug wool so that it will cross and cover the wide horizontal channels of the double-mesh canvas. However, in stitching the rug wool into the canvas, your needle comes up through and goes down into the narrow vertical channels. The pattern of over-and-under stitches is alternated one row after the other.

In weaving done on a loom, the warp and the weft would be pushed together to form a strong material. Here the support of the needlepoint canvas allows us to see very clearly the simple over–under effect of tabby weaving.

This technique has tremendous possibilities. You can make up different woven surfaces by changing the pattern—size and repetition—of your over-and-under stitches. You can also add other materials.

Mysterious Islands is a design that suits itself to relatively little planning ahead as far as color is concerned. Choose a wide range of colors and just decide what color you will use predominantly. Then use the other colors in obviously smaller areas, making up the shapes with your needle as you go. If you are using a pale main color, as I did, then choose darker colors so that their forms will show up. If you choose a dark main color, choose paler colors for contrast. Then have fun letting your needle do the work!

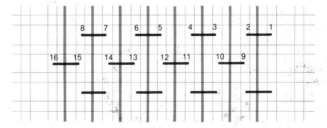

Fig. 72. Tramé crossed by Running Stitches on double-mesh rug canvas.

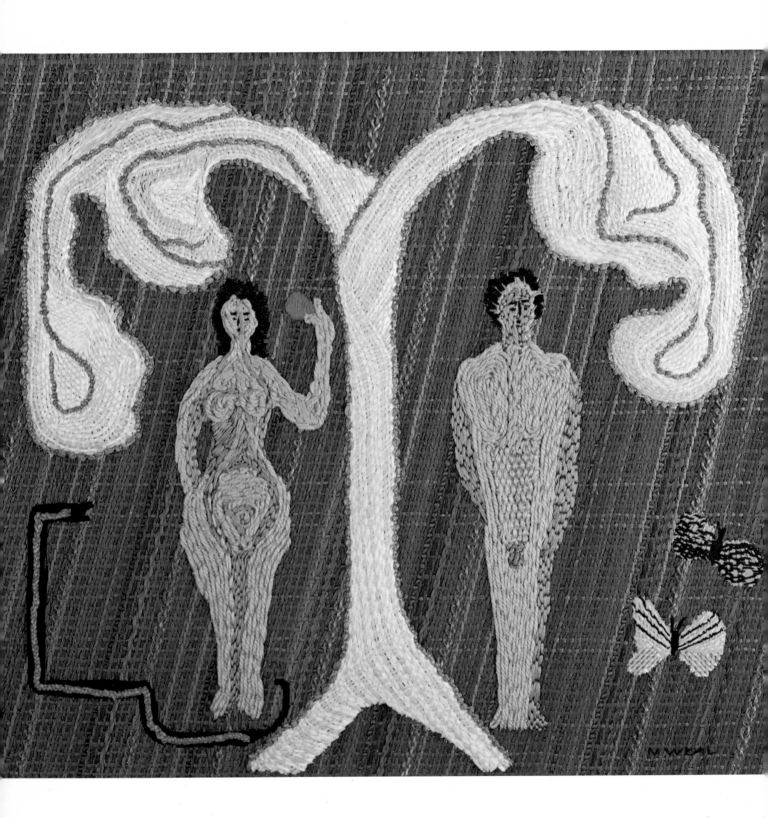

94

Plate 29. Adam and Eve Wall Hanging.

ADAM AND EVE WALL HANGING

[Color Plates 25, 29 through 36]

As I experimented with techniques for using colors in layers, I began to think of Tramé as a foundation—a warp or weft—upon which I could interlink and intertwine embroidery and needleweaving stitches. (*See* Color Plates **32** and **33**, Photo 33.)

In my approach to integrating needlepoint with embroidery and needleweaving, I do not first fill the needlepoint canvas with Tent Stitching—in an attempt to make an embroidery material—and then embroider on that. Instead, I try to integrate directly whatever technique and stitch I am using, so that embroidery or needleweaving fits in or is locked into the whole texture of the design. You might call this technique collage or appliqué of various textures and materials that I make myself. The difference is that the varied textures are not glued or stitched together. The different textures are made in their appropriate shapes and colors on the needlepoint canvas itself.

The Adam and Eve Wall Hanging is done on No. 10 mono canvas, using Persian yarn, tapestry wool, and various types of linens, silk, and cotton. It was worked on a floor frame. Its dimensions are 37 x 27½ inches.

A variation of a familiar needlepoint stitch, the Renaissance Stitch (Fig. 73), is literally at the bottom of the Adam and Eve Wall Hanging.

In Fig. 73 the red indicates the Tramé. The black indicates the Upright Gobelin Stitch which is done over the Tramé. When these two stitches are combined in this fashion, the result is called the Renaissance Stitch.

The Renaissance Stitch is used in the traditional way in the Staircase, a detail of which is shown in Photo 34. In this case, the Tramé does not show through. It is used as padding so that the flowers and leaves, which are done in Persian yarn and linen,

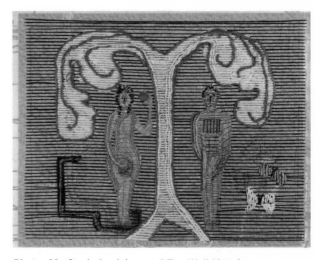

Photo 33. Study for Adam and Eve Wall Hanging.

stand out from the Tent Stitch background. (*See* Color Plate **48**.)

I changed the Renaissance Stitch to use it as the background foundation in the Adam and Eve Wall Hanging. Fig. 74 shows the foundation in diagram form. (*See also* Color Plate **32**.) The Tramé is shown in red in Fig. 74. In the actual piece, it was laid with blue, violet, and blue-green 3-ply Persian yarn used in long lengths, crossing the entire width of the canvas, a row length at a time. These long lengths of Persian yarn were tied down by the Upright Gobelin Stitches in the pattern shown in Fig. 74. The diagonal channels between the Upright Gobelin Stitches were filled in with various embroidery stitches and techniques. The tied-down Tramé bars are used as the Laid Work foundation of the stitches. The Raised Band Chain Stitch (Fig. 75), Whipped Spider Web (Figs. 76a and 76b), braiding and freehand forms of weaving over and under the Tramé bars were used.

Plate 30. Detail of Eve in Adam and Eve Wall Hanging.

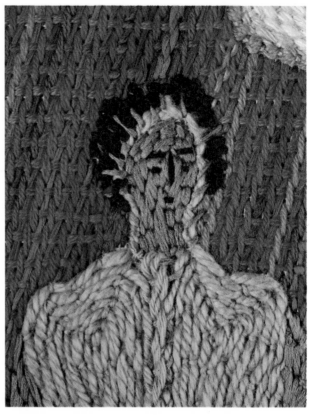

Plate 31. Detail of Adam in Adam and Eve Wall Hanging.

Plate 32. Detail of foundation of background of Adam and Eve Wall Hanging.

Plate 33. Detail of background of Adam and Eve Wall Hanging.

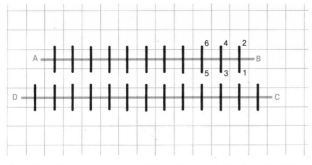

Fig. 73. The Renaissance Stitch: the upright Gobelin Stitch over Tramé.

Photo 34. Detail of flower from Staircase, showing a traditional use of the Renaissance Stitch.

Fig. 74. Background foundation of Adam and Eve Wall Hanging.

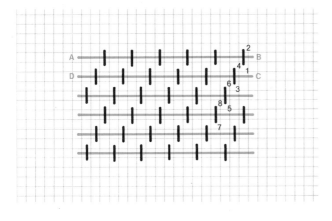

Fig. 75. Raised Band Chain Stitch.

The background texture of the Adam and Eve Wall Hanging would make a handsome decorative pillow.

Directions for a simplified version of the background are given on page 98.

The Adam and Eve Wall Hanging develops relief and sculptural qualities as the height and depth of areas are extensively varied. I sculpted the figures of Adam and Eve by using Medieval Couching and Basic Couching and French Knots. I also used free-hand needleweaving and stitching. The tree was done with free-form needleweaving and outlined with Loop Couching.

The butterflies have crenellated and creviced textures. The butterfly in Color Plate **34** is done in three layers: a base of close Satin Stitches, then bars, then Detached Cretan Stitches. The butterfly in Color Plate **35** is done in several layers of needleweaving over and under expanded Renaissance Stitches. The snake (Color Plate **36**) is worked with long stitches as a foundation and then compressed Detached Cretan Stitches are used over that.

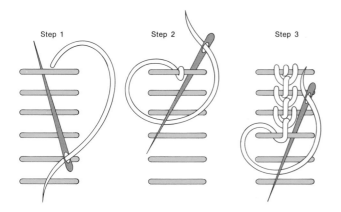

Step 1   Step 2   Step 3

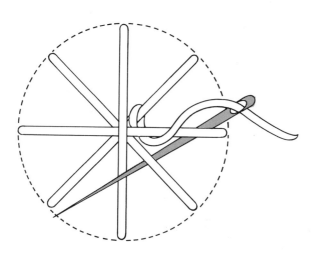

Fig. 76a. Whipped Spider Web.

Plate 34. Detail of butterfly from Adam and Eve Wall Hanging.

Fig. 76b. Whipped Spider Web done in a straight line.

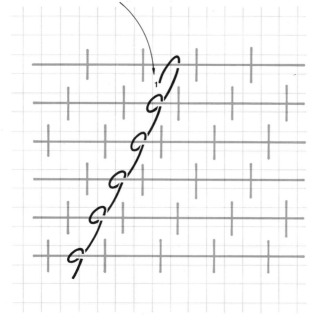

Needle comes up at 1 and does not enter material again until channel is finished or thread is used up.

Directions for Background Texture

MATERIALS:

    No. 10 mono canvas
    Persian yarn
    Tapestry wool
    Embroidery linens, cottons, and silks

■ Set up the background foundation, working from Fig. 74. Use 3-ply Persian yarn.

■ Fill out the dimensions of your canvas by repeating the following pattern as many times as necessary. Determine on practice canvas the ply or thickness necessary for whatever materials you choose to use.

Channel 1: Pull yarn under the foundation bars.

Channel 2: Pull yarn under the foundation bars.

Channel 3: Use Raised Band Chain Stitch (Fig. 75).

Channel 4: Whipped Spider Web (Fig. 76b) goes over every bar.

Channel 5: Pull yarn under the foundation bars.

Channel 6: Whipped Spider Web over every other bar —weaving over the intervening bars.

Channel 7: Use Raised Band Chain Stitch.

Plate 35. Detail of butterfly from Adam and Eve Wall Hanging.

Plate 36. Detail of snake from Adam and Eve Wall Hanging.

Learning Needleweaving

If you decide to experiment with woven and sculptural techniques in needlepoint, keep in mind that it is not necessary for you to know anything about weaving, as we generally think of it, on a loom. Many embroidery stitches are detached and involve what really is needleweaving. Stitchery and weaving techniques are closely related.

Familiarize yourself with some of the simple embroidery stitches illustrated in this book and with others that you may know or learn. Good books to consult include *Stitchery for Children,* by Jacqueline Enthoven; *Adventures in Stitches,* by Mariska Karasz; *The Complete Guide to Embroidery Stitches and Crewel,* by Jo Bucher; and *Erica Wilson's Embroidery Book.* The Bibliography beginning on page 173 lists these and other excellent information sources.

Practice attached and detached stitches on the usual woven embroidery materials first—in as free a manner as possible. Photos 35a–h show details from some of my samplers. Remember—if you can do a simple over-and-under Running Stitch you can do needleweaving.

When you work with embroidery techniques on canvas, just think of the needlepoint canvas as a very open or loose embroidery foundation. Do not think or worry about counting boxes and threads.

In general, I prefer to use tapestry wool when doing embroidery stitches on needlepoint canvas. The fact that tapestry wool is not made up of ply, and therefore does not split, makes it easier to handle. Nevertheless, there are times when I do use Persian yarn instead.

As much as I love woven materials, I prefer to weave with a needle rather than with a loom. To me, there is more variety of movement when one stitches and uses a needle. Of course, there are things that can be done in weaving that you cannot do in needlepoint, and vice versa. I prefer needlepoint and needleweaving because I feel in closer contact with my materials. There is no loom or piece of machinery between me and my creation.

Photos 35a–h. DETAILS FROM EMBROIDERY SAMPLERS.

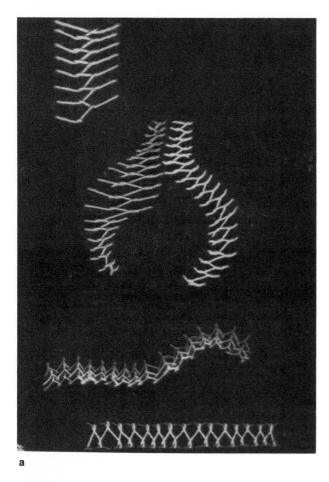

a

c

d

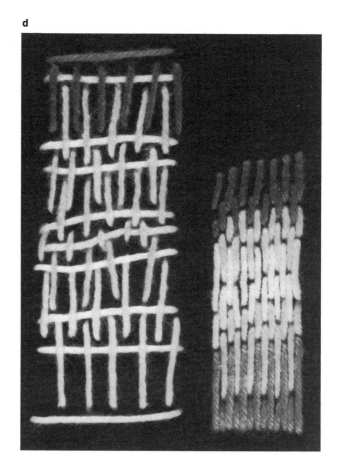

b

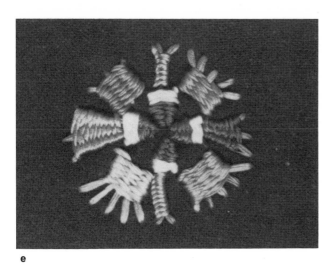

e

f

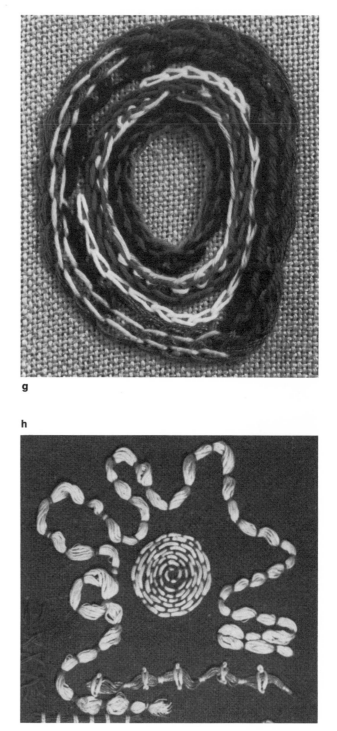

g

h

TWO

Color

Preliminary Remarks about Color

Color is a vast and fascinating subject. In preparing this section, I asked myself: "What can I tell you, what do I know about color, what have I found from my work, that will help in the needlepoint designing you may do?"

In choosing from the broad and numerous approaches to color those areas and those aspects that will be most helpful, I have drawn on my experience in working for and with people who love needlepoint. I have analyzed, as clearly as I can, how I handle color.

It is not easy for me to write clearly and honestly about color; some statements may seem contradictory. Remember that color is an area filled with ambiguities and variations in perception.

Perhaps the deeper, more sophisticated understanding of color, as well as everything else in life, does mean that we have to accept what seem to be contradictions.

Some things I do instinctively with color, yet I cannot explain, specifically, certain of my reactions to colors. Each of us has a personal response to color, and probably the only way to share it with another individual is by the actual use of color, the actual needlepoint we do.

Nevertheless, I consciously make use of some definite principles concerning color in my designing and work with color and stitches. The Mini-Course in Color Fundamentals which follows summarizes those principles. Particular designs will illustrate how I make use of my color knowledge.

But first I want to encourage you as much as possible to think freely about color.

The single most important fact to know about color is that it is an emotional, expressive, and deeply instinctive area. Encouraging you to cultivate your own personal response to colors of all kinds, used in all kinds of ways, is the first and most important help that I can offer. Motivating you to think freely

about color will, I hope, be a worthwhile and valuable contribution of this book. I would hate to do anything that might keep you from sensing that colors are mysterious, exciting and powerful.

No one can teach you to feel color; I can only encourage you to do so. No one can teach you how to respond to color, I can only encourage you to accept your response and enjoy it. I would not presume to tell you how you should respond to any group of colors or any design. Trust your instinct, just as I trust mine. If you look at and work with color, with the desire to feel it, you will.

People love to see and respond to unusual and expressive color use; yet, for some reason, they are timid about using color themselves. Many sensitive, perceptive, and responsive persons are held back by a color shyness, a fear of committing some grievous color sin.

Even for the bold, color choice can be a problem area. Many people who do needlepoint develop a greater proficiency and imagination in the use of stitches. You learn by practicing them on various types of canvases with different types of wools and threads. Naturally you respond and bit by bit you gain confidence in your stitch and texture sense and use.

Clients come to me and say: "You know, I am beginning to feel quite confident about doing the stitches. I think I can even make up my own designs, my own textures. But I still need help with color. I'm really not sure of myself with color. I am afraid of making mistakes. I know what I like and what I don't like, but that doesn't seem to help when I am selecting colors for a needlepoint piece. I'd like to use color interestingly, but I don't really know where to start."

The main reason many who do needlepoint have difficulty with color choice is that they have come into this artistic medium through familiarity and experimentation with stitches and textures. My experience was the reverse: I started out by learning about color and painting, and then went into an in-depth study of stitchery and textures.

Thus, the person experiencing difficulty with color may not be as pragmatically aware of the structure of color as about the structure—the contrasts and similarities—of stitches. Most needleworkers have not had training or experience in mixing paints to produce colors.

It is important to remember that even though needlepoint artists spend a good deal of time working with color, they differ from painters, who also devote themselves to color use, in a striking way. Needlepoint artists, in contrast to painters, do not have to make their own colors.

The work of mixing pigment or dye, to obtain innumerable colors or shades, is done for you. However, this shortcut can make your color choice more difficult. Unless you consciously think about it, you may completely ignore relating and contrasting colors in terms of their structure. Making use of contrast and similarity in colors is just as important as it is in texture!

Your job in needlepoint, and mine, is to choose colors from those that are available, and make our designs as effective and as artistically pleasing as possible.

To do this, it is necessary to know some basics about color, the fundamentals such as I learned from painting. The needlepoint worker or artist need not be disadvantaged by a lack of color knowledge. The Mini-Course in Color Fundamentals that follows specifically relates color theory to needlepoint.

Plate 37. Stars and Stripes Belt.

Mini-Course in Color Fundamentals

This Mini-Course in Color Fundamentals has been planned as a basic reference. Read through it once, and immediately begin to use as much of it as you can. As you continue to work with color in needlepoint, you will come back many times to this Mini-Course to expand your knowledge and your color horizons.

Fig. 77 shows a color wheel.[13] The central circle shows yellow, red, and blue—the color primaries. They are called primaries because every other color that exists in some way derives from a mixture of these three.

The three secondary colors—green, orange, and violet—are shown in the middle circle. A secondary is formed by mixing together two of the primaries. In other words:

> Yellow and red make orange.
> Red and blue make violet.
> Blue and yellow make green.

The outer circle shows in diagram form what happens when a primary is mixed with a secondary. The resulting color is a mixture of both and is therefore related to both. It is called a tertiary. Naturally, in the color wheel, a tertiary stands between a primary and a secondary. You can see that if you mix a green (secondary) with a yellow (primary) you will produce a yellow-green (tertiary).

The three big signposts, or common denominators, of the colors are red, yellow, and blue, and in secondary or auxiliary position, orange, violet, and green.

The color scheme of the Stars and Stripes Belt (Color Plate 37) is based on the three primary colors used with white. The stripes are red, white, and blue; the stars are yellow and white.

Color Contrast 1[14]

Colors contrast and relate according to chroma, hue, or quality.

When thinking about color, I very often think in terms of the color wheel, because it clearly shows how colors vary and contrast in chroma quality and effect.[15]

A yellow may be made redder or bluer.
A red may be made yellower or bluer.
A blue may be made redder or yellower.
A green may be made bluer or yellower.
A violet may be made redder or bluer.
An orange may be made yellower or redder.[16]

The color wheel also expresses admirably how the colors are related. Using the color wheel, it is easy to think of color as progressing from yellow to red, then from red to blue, then from blue to green, and finally from green back to yellow, the original starting point.[17]

This color contrast is important for the needlepoint worker. Since we do not make or mix our own colors, we have to be able to recognize and feel hue or chroma quality.

We have a wide assortment of colors from which to choose. As I look at each color at my disposal, I automatically think: Is this basically a yellow? Is this basically a red? Is this basically a blue? I try to respond to every color, whether it is neutral or intense, in terms of its chroma quality. And that means that I ask myself: Does it have a lot of yellow in it, or a little? Does it have a lot of red, or a little? Does it have a lot of blue, or a little?

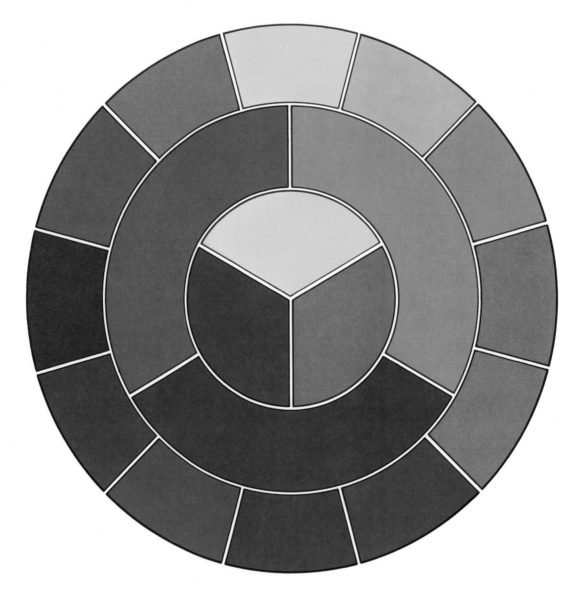

Fig. 77. The color wheel.

Color Contrast 2

*Two colors can be in a warm–cool
relationship to each other.*

We can sense the quality of two colors in terms of
warmth and coolness. This is a color contrast that I
constantly make use of.

The greatest cold–warm contrast effect is obtained
with the colors orange-red and blue-green in juxtaposition.[18] A sense of coolness is usually experienced
if a color has more blue-green in it. A sense of warmness is usually experienced if a color has more red-
orange in it.

You can start to sense warmness and coolness in
colors by asking yourself: How does this color appear
next to the color I see it with? Does it appear to have
more red-orange in it? If so, it will have the effect of
a warm color. Does it appear to have more blue-green
in it? In that case, it will have a relatively cool effect.

The sensitive needlepoint designer takes advantage
of the fact that there are contrasts of warmth and
coolness between colors. I always at least consider
contrasting a warm and cool version of the same hue.
It can be very interesting and effective to compare
or contrast a cool pink with a warm pink as in Mountain Peaks, Variation 2 (Color Plate 16).

You can also contrast a cool color, a blue, for instance, with a warm shade of a different hue, such as
red. In the Adam and Eve Stool, the warm red apple
is in contrast to the cool blue night sky (Color Plates
1 and 2).

Color Contrast 3

Each color has its opposite or complement.

The color that is most opposite or different from yellow is violet, because relatively little yellow has gone
into the composition of violet.

The color that is most different from red is green,
because relatively little red has gone into the composition of green.

The color that is most different from orange is blue,
because hardly any blue has gone into the composition
of orange.

You can use the color wheel to determine quickly
color opposites or complements. In the color circle,
the outer disk of the diagram, the complementary
colors stand opposite each other. Just draw an invisible
diameter through the center of the circle from one
color to its opposite.

It is important to know the complements or color
opposites. When two complements are placed side
by side they intensify each other and make each other
appear more brilliant. Lattice Work, Variation 2
(Color Plate 38) is based on the complementary
relationship of red and green.

Oddly enough, if you mix two complements together to produce a new color, you will get a gray or
a brown, a neutral. Mixed together, the two complements will destroy each other.

An interesting color contrast can be achieved by
putting a color with its split-complement, not its
complement.

The split-complements are the two colors that are

Plate 38. Lattice Work, Variation 2.

found on either side of a color's complement. In other words, the split-complements of yellow would be blue-violet and red-violet. I used these split-complements to construct Patchwork I, Variation 2 (Color Plate 5).

The design of the Pocketbook is based on the use of the split-complements yellow and blue-violet. The background of one side, Orpheus Charming the Beasts (Color Plate 39), is yellow. The dominant background color of the other side, Jason Returns with the Golden Fleece (Color Plate 40), is blue-violet.

The split-complements orange and blue-green are used to construct Lattice Work, Color Version 1 (Color Plate 9).

I used complementary and split-complementary colors to shade the Cat Pillow. The head of the cat is predominantly yellow, yellow-orange, and orange. In addition to using deeper shades of the oranges to attain color variation, I used blues and blue-violets (Color Plate 26).

Color Contrast 4

Colors can be intense or they can be dull in relation to each other.

Intensity–dullness is another color contrast that I make great use of.

You can make a color less intense—in other words, duller, muddier, and grayer—by mixing in its complement, or one of its split-complements, or by adding white or black.

Putting red into a green will create a muddy brown. Mixing orange into blue will create a muddy dark green, and mixing violet and yellow can produce brownish green.

Browns can be yellowish, reddish, bluish, or greenish. Some grays are greener than others; there are also reddish grays and yellowish grays. Browns and grays are just dull forms of more intense colors. Think of a brilliant color, such as a strong blue, as simply an intense or highly chromatic form of a gray.

Plate 39. Orpheus Charming the Beasts, one side of pocketbook design.

Plate 40. Jason Returns with the Golden Fleece, on the other side of the pocketbook.

Intensity–dullness is an important color contrast. If you are using all intense colors in a design, a muddy or dull color will give the eye some needed relief and variety. In addition, you can make your brilliant colors appear more intense by comparing them with a muddy color. And the muddy color attains, in my eye anyway, a special glow!

This is the approach I used in the Adam and Eve Wall Hanging (Color Plates 25 and 29 through 36). The Wall Hanging is composed of intense colors: blue, orange, white, yellow, and black. For the figures of Adam and Eve, I used a relatively dull or muddy color—yellow ochre.

Instead of stressing intense colors, you can build a design with predominantly neutral colors—ochres, browns, and grays—and then use a small amount of one or two intense colors. You will see how they sing.

I used this approach for the Man's Tennis Racquet Cover (Photo 36). The background is neutral tan and most of the features are done in black, which, in this case, plays the role of a neutral. The pupils are blue and the mouth is rust brown.

Color Contrast 5

Colors can be opposed or contrasted by using color areas of different sizes.

This color contrast means that color has measure.[19] You can measure with your eye the amount of any particular color in a design. A color can extend way far out, it can occupy the whole area of a design, or it can be used as a dot, in the tiniest amount imaginable.

Try to think about and feel the effect of a small amount of color in relation to a larger amount of another color. If you use a great deal of blue and a little bit of yellow, that yellow will appear different than if you had used the same yellow in a great amount and a little bit of the same blue. Try to think about and visualize the effects of different colors if they are used in equal areas or if they are used in unequal areas.

Photo 36. Man's Tennis Racquet Cover.

Sometimes when I run into trouble with color, it may be that I have inadvertently allowed myself to use too many evenly balanced color areas in one piece. That is, the areas of the different colors are too nearly equal in size. To avoid this make sure that one color is clearly dominant, and that the other colors can be seen in clearly differing, smaller amounts.[20]

Let's suppose we are making a design based on chroma contrast, using red, blue, yellow, and green. Choose one of these colors to occupy the greatest amount of space, and then use each of the other colors in clearly smaller amounts, each of the smaller amounts being different one from the other. What color occupies the largest amount of space, what color the next largest, and so on, should be readily apparent.

The Adam and Eve Wall Hanging (Color Plate 29) exemplifies this rule. The largest amount of color is the blue background. The next largest is white, then the ochre of the figures, then the yellow of the butterflies. The least amount of color is the red for the apple (incidentally, this is deliberate—to draw attention to the apple). I tried to draw the design so that each color occupied a clearly differing amount of space measurable accurately by eye.

You may recall that same rule in relation to using different textures in one piece, as explained on page 34. Make it clear which texture dominates, and try to use the other or others in clearly smaller and differing amounts.

Color Contrast 6

Two colors have a color effect on each other.

You may think that, since red and yellow make orange, if you put a red area next to a yellow area in your needlepoint design, you will get an overall orangish effect. This is not what happens and this color misconception is at the heart of many problems in color use.

What really happens is that the two colors interact with each other. The red, in our example, tends to pull the redness out of the yellowness, and therefore makes the yellow look greener or more like yellow-green. The yellow, for its part, tends to pull the yellowness out of the red, and therefore pushes the red toward violet, and makes the red appear more like a red-violet.

The color wheel can be used to determine the effect two colors, used side by side, will have on each other. Choose any two colors that are not in a complementary relationship to each other. Each pure color physiologically demands its opposite color or complementary.[21] If it is not present in the design to see, the eye produces it—a phenomenon known as simultaneous contrast.

Another way of saying this is: Two colors that are not in a complementary relationship to each other will tend to move themselves into a complementary relationship.

For example, if you put a blue-green next to a blue, the blue-green will look greener or more like a green, and the blue will look more like a blue-violet. Instead of mixing together in effect, two colors, side by side, will appear to move away from each other toward a complementary relationship on the color wheel.

Knowing about this color contrast will help you to match any color. For example, a client might select a red from my wools to show me the color of her sofa. And yet, that same red she herself chose, when put into the design with the other colors used, may not look like the sofa color at all! Therefore, when a color that should be matching doesn't seem to match in the design context, I always start to think about simultaneous contrast, the technical name for this color effect.

Simultaneous contrast is an important color fundamental for the needlepoint designer. We must see and use our colors side by side, and so this color contrast is almost always in action. Remember that the quality or effect of a color can and does change as it is used with another color.

If the blue-green used in Lattice Work—where it is used with oranges and greens—were put with a red, it would appear different to the eye; it would have a different color effect. You can see in Lattice Work (Color Plate 9) how different the deep orange bands appear next to the orange and green diamonds from the way they do next to the blue-green diamonds. The deep orange bands seem to glow and vibrate next to the blue-green. They appear duller and more matt in quality next to the orange and the green.

Making Color Studies for Designs

Carry this principle over to your own needlepoint color work. Be sure you always try out, in some way or another, the colors you are planning to use. Remember: Once colors become part of a visual design, the unity of the design becomes the most important factor to consider.

There are many ways to try out colors. A simple one is to take some pieces of wool and roll them into shapes approximating the eventual areas. Place the wools in positions similar to those they are to occupy in the design. You will be able to judge very clearly the effect of one on the other. Even if you paint your design, always try the wools next to each other.

If you wish to be even more exact, you can, as I do, make sketches on practice canvas, using large and bold stitches to show the colored wools you are contemplating (Photo 37). My study for Patchwork I, Variation 2 (Color Plate 5) was stitched out on a scrap of embroidery material (Photo 39).

Or quickly sketch pastel impressions of the stitches on solid-color paper that matches your background color, as shown in Photo 38.

An acrylic color study may be made using an acetate overlay indicating the stitches to be used (Photo 40).

It is pointless, as far as I am concerned, to decide to use any particular color without trying it next to the color you are going to use it with. Every color changes in its effect, depending upon the other color or colors with which it is used. And most important of all, you must let your eye, not your head, judge your color use and color choices.

If you took the blue background of the Adam and Eve Wall Hanging (Color Plates 29 and 33) and put it in another color context, say browns, whites, grays, and pinks, it might look quite handsome, but it would look different.

It is not so important that you know precisely what happens or why it happens. Just try to develop a sensitivity to the fact that the effect a color has on your eye is dependent upon the color context it is in, and that the effect is not necessarily a blending or mixing.

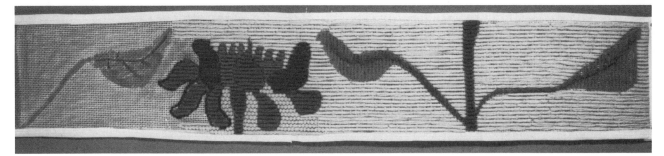

Photo 37. Study for staircase riser.

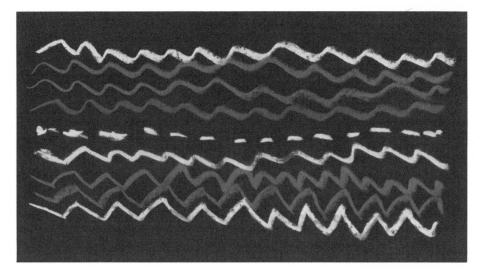

Photo 38. Pastel study on solid-color paper in background color.

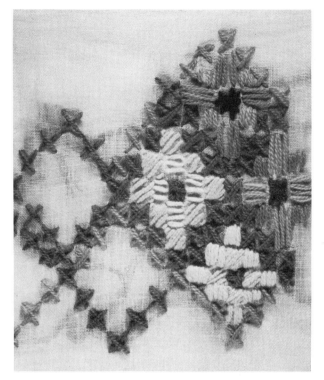

Photo 39. Study for Patchwork I, Variation 2, was stitched on scrap of embroidery material.

Photo 40. Acrylic color study uses acetate overlay to indicate stitches.

Color Contrast 7

Colors can be compared in terms of paleness or lightness, darkness or heaviness.

This color contrast principle has been saved for the last in the Mini-Course because it is such an important one for the needleworker. I also wish to go into it at greater length than the previous contrasts. I use this color contrast in every design.

I like to respond to color, and I like to allow myself to free-associate with it. Color, of all the visual elements, is perhaps most able to inspire and motivate. The use of color can set a mood and evoke an atmosphere.[22] Color can be expressive of emotion and feeling, and human beings are known to respond physically and emotionally to color and color effects.

We respond emotionally to paleness and darkness in color. A design composed primarily of heavy dark colors might make you feel sadness, depth, and vibrancy; whereas a design composed essentially of light colors might make you feel delicacy, optimism, and spaciousness.

Experimenting with color is part of the pleasure of needlepoint. I like to try putting next to each other whatever colors come to mind, to see what the effect will be. I like to let myself go with color, to make use of the color contrasts.

I find that following my instinct is as a rule the very best approach, but sometimes I think I get hung up on my own emotional reaction to color. Something doesn't look quite right, and then I try various possibilities by trial and error or even in desperation until my studio floor is covered with pulled-out pieces of wool.

When I find myself in this kind of quandary, I try to think about colors in a more detached way. Instead of concentrating on or emphasizing the expressive, emotional and physical intensities and qualities of the colors I am working with, I try to forget that my colors are colors at all.

I think of the colors I am using in terms of black, white, and gray. I concentrate on Color Contrast 7 and think of the colors only in terms of their lightness and heaviness. To think of colors in terms of their relative weight you must translate whatever colors you are using into their black, white, and gray equivalencies.

All colors have weight.[23] They have lightness or heaviness, paleness or darkness. The term *value* refers to the lightness or darkness of a color.[24]

If you want paler and lighter colors, just add some white. If you want deeper and darker colors, just add some black. For instance, we can take a red and keep adding white, and we will get a lighter and lighter color. If we keep adding black to red, we will get a deeper and deeper color.

Most needleworkers are familiar with this aspect of color, although they may have used it in only a limited way. We are all accustomed to working with, for example, a light blue, a middle blue, and a dark blue, to produce traditional light–dark shading effects. And we all know that most embroidery and needlepoint wools and threads come in families, or groupings, of lighter and darker shades of any particular color.

The colors themselves—yellow, red, blue, orange, violet, and green—have different relative weights or values. Adding yellow to a Kelly green gives a lighter and more yellow green. There are significant differences in value or depth between colors as we see them on the color wheel or on a shade card. These value differences are very important to become aware of, to consider, and to use.

It is easy to see that a certain blue has a lot of white in it, and is very much lighter than a blue that has a great deal of black in it. This approach can be extended so that when you see a yellow next to a purple, you think to yourself: Which color is lighter or paler? Which color is heavier or darker?

It is difficult to judge completely accurately with the naked eye the lightness and darkness of relative colors.[25] Which is lighter, for instance—a royal blue or a scarlet red?

But even in difficult comparisons it is advisable to make a decision. At least the effort to do so will enable you to know whether or not there is a clear light–dark contrast between two or more colors. You will be able to choose colors that are clearly different, or if you wish, you will be able to choose colors that are very close to each other in terms of paleness and darkness.

Any mistakes you make in this area will not be tragic. Any attempt to see and use light–dark contrast will help you in designing.

One way to achieve more color variety in designing is directly related to this fact. Since I compare colors in terms of blackness, whiteness, and grayness, I also think of blacks, whites, and grays as colors themselves, and use them with my other colors. Look for and use whites that have traces of blues, pinks, and yellows in them. Look for and use blacks that seem to have a touch of green, blue, or even red. Start to think of grays in terms of their color content.

The fact that colors have lightness and darkness is proved by the very existence of black-and-white photography. Look at any one of the black-and-white photographs in this book. When the color version of that design was photographed in black and white, it became a black, gray, and white design. Each and every color in relation one to the other has not only a chroma quality but a value of lightness and darkness, which is easily seen in black-and-white photographs.

The needlepoint artist, as well as the painter, spends a great deal of time in learning how to judge the relative value of colors. Artists and designers learn to judge colors in terms of black, white, and gray without using a black-and-white camera.

Using the Value Scale

One reason lightness–darkness is such an important color contrast is that because of it, we are able to set up a value scale (Fig. 78). This scale is shown in terms of black, white, and gray. The same thing can be done with any color; for example, with red, going from the deepest reddish black to the palest pink. You can make a value scale for groups of different colors, showing the darkest, the lightest, and those in between.

The number 1 represents a white or the lightest color in the group; 9, the deepest color. The scale shows that one can go from the whitest, lightest color to a darker gray or color, until one finally reaches the deepest and heaviest color.

The 1 could just as easily represent a very pale blue or a white with a trace of blue in it. The 9 could be a heavy blue or a black with traces of blue in it.

The 1 could also represent a pale yellow, and the 9 could stand for a deep and heavy violet.

All the numbers in between 1 and 9 represent the grays that occur when mixing together different amounts of black and white. These numbers also represent the various shades of blue that would occur if you mixed light blue with deep blue.

The numbers 1 through 9 can also represent the various colors of a multi-hue design, in terms of lightness and darkness.

Just as I habitually use the color wheel, I also make great use of the value scale. Much trial-and-error experience has taught me to think about the light–dark contrasts of color from the moment I start selecting my colors. I usually line up my colors from the deepest to the lightest, and number them in my mind according to the numbers on the value scale. In other words, I translate my colors into black, white, and gray equivalencies.[26]

Numbering my colors in terms of the value scale, and laying them out before me, going from the lightest to the darkest, makes it easy to use many colors in one design. I make sure I have not chosen all deep shades in one design, or all pale shades. I make sure that there is some variation of lightness and darkness between my colors, and then try to use that variation to construct the pattern of the design.

Value Scale

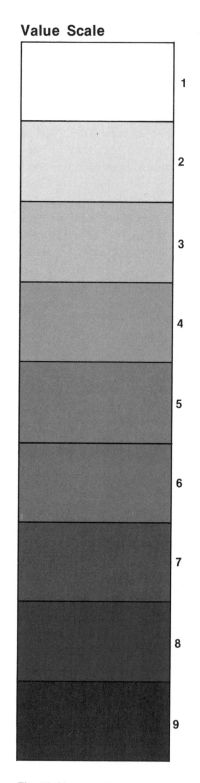

Fig. 78. Value scale.

In Lattice Work (Photo 41 and Color Plate 10) six values are used: 1, 2, 3, 4, 8, and 9. The deep blue is the darkest color used, so I call it 9. The two whites are the lightest, but there is a difference in value between them, so the pinker white is 2 and the bluer white is 1. There is such a slight difference in value between the two yellows in this design that in the overall scheme they appeared to me to occupy the same position in the scale, so I call them both 3. The pale blue is deeper than the whites, but lighter than the yellows, so it is called 2.

In Spectrum I (Color Plate 41), I chose different colors but arranged them in a sequence according to their value equivalencies. The value numbers are given in Photo 42 so that you can get a feeling for laying out colors going from the deepest to the lightest. This pillow was done in seven completely different colors—red-violet, red, orange, yellow, green, blue, blue-violet—the colors of the spectrum or color wheel.

Spectrum I can also be done in seven shades of one color, creating a monochromatic design (Color Plate 42). In that case, put the darkest shade at the left and go in sequence all the way across the pillow to the lightest shade at the right.

A versatile pillow, Spectrum I can be done in all kinds of color combinations and it fits well into traditional as well as contemporary settings. Some of my clients have used two Spectrum I pillows in the same colors on their sofas, as backdrops for other smaller needlepoint pillows.

Spectrum I evolved from my experimentation with the Darning Stitch on No. 3 mono rug canvas. The Darning Stitch works beautifully on this type of canvas because it is a bold and dramatic stitch. Using large-mesh canvas with heavy wool really shows the Darning Stitch to great advantage.

Do the Darning Stitch over 2 and 5 canvas threads as shown in Fig. 79a. A border of two rows of Cross Stitching all around Spectrum I finishes it off nicely. At the top and bottom edges a row of Back Stitching fits between the Cross Stitches and the Darning Stitches (Fig. 79b). On the sides of the pillow, put in a row of Straight Gobelin Stitches (do them horizontally or turn the canvas) before the Cross Stitching. Then Back Stitch between the Straight Gobelin Stitches and the Cross Stitches as shown in Fig. 79c.

Photo 41. Lattice Work, Color Version 2. (Colors are numbered in terms of the Value Scale.)

Plate 41. Spectrum I, Color Version 1.

Photo 42. Spectrum I. (Colors are numbered in terms of the Value Scale.)

Photo 43. Detail of edge of Spectrum I.

Plate 42. Spectrum I, Color Version 2.

Using Color Chords

Thinking in terms of black, white, and gray enables one to see clearly and to consider the intervals or value spaces that exist between colors. The interval between values helps us to distinguish between them. Well-structured color design is related to the use of value intervals. By utilizing two intervals, or three different values, one can strike a chord. The needle-point artist has an infinite number of color chords at his disposal.

For instance, in choosing three colors in a design, you could select colors whose lightness and darkness— or value—translation would correspond to 1, 5, and 9 on the value scale (Fig. 80). The imaginary value space between the 1 and the 5 and between the 5 and the 9 is called the interval. If in your design you place whatever color is 1 next to whatever color is 9, you will also be using the interval 1, 9. Intervals can be repeated or varied, according to your taste and judg-

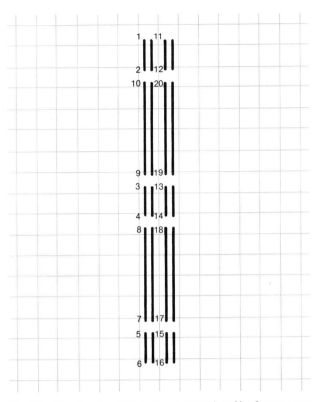

Fig. 79a. The Darning Stitch. Use rug wool on No. 3 mono rug canvas.

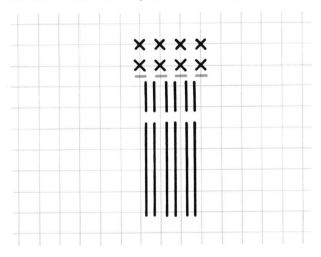

Fig. 79b. The top and bottom edges of Spectrum I, showing two rows of Cross Stitching and Back Stitching.

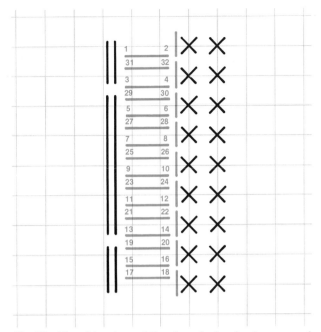

Fig. 79c. The side edges of Spectrum I, showing two rows of Cross Stitching, Back Stitching, and the Upright Gobelin Stitch (done horizontally).

ment, as well as what you consider to be the needs of each design's structure.

Fig. 80 shows a possible color chord, with possible color choices. If you wish to orchestrate it—put more color into a design based on this chord—you reason this way: Maroon (red) and yellow make a sort of orange, and therefore I can use an orange whose value is between 1 and 5, say 3. The desirable orange thus is deeper than the yellow and lighter than the olive.

To select still another color, you might continue: Maroon (red) and olive (green) mixed together make a brownish gray. Therefore, I will choose a brownish gray whose value is between 5 and 9, say 7; that is, darker than the olive, but lighter than the maroon.

Try choosing colors for a design based on a chord using three different values. Orchestrate that chord in a manner similar to the one just described. You will discover that it is fun to work this way and you will find yourself coming up with interesting and unusual color combinations. Also, your work will be well designed from the color point of view.

Fig. 80 shows a color chord based on rather large intervals. Color chords can be based on intervals that are much closer together, such as 1, 2, 3, as in Fig. 81. Spectrum I (Photo 42, page 118) is based on the color chord suggested in Fig. 81.

Understanding color in terms of black, white, and gray values will enable you to use the photographs in this or any other book as patterns for your own color variations. As you analyze each black-and-white photo and each color plate, you will be on your way to structuring your own color versions with clear value intervals, chords, or sequences. Now as you select colors by their approximate value equivalents, you can deepen and enrich your color choice by experimenting with and using the other color contrasts.

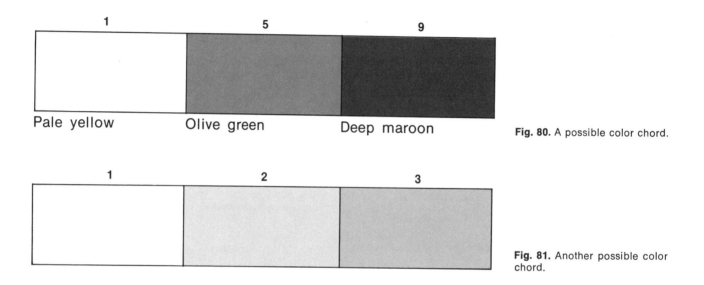

1   **5**   **9**

Pale yellow   Olive green   Deep maroon

Fig. 80. A possible color chord.

1   **2**   **3**

Fig. 81. Another possible color chord.

Shading

A great deal of needlepoint has been designed from the light–dark shading point of view. Everybody is familiar with the pieces of needlepoint available in stores: You shade the leaf by putting darkened tones of green on its outer contours. This is, of course, an abbreviated or shorthand version of chiaroscuro.[27]

You can shade by using lighter and darker tones of the same color; you can also shade by using lighter and darker tones of different colors. Through shading one can achieve color variation.

Shading can be done in several ways. You can put different tones or shades side by side: Wells Fargo Man's Belt (Photo 44) is done in that fashion, as is Byzantine Jewels, No. 3 (Color Plate 20). Or you can merge one tone into another. Some of the Golf Course Vest (Color Plate 43) is done in that way.

In the vest, you can see the various ways that I used shading and the Tent Stitch. The vest was worked on No. 18 mono canvas with 1-ply Persian yarn.

As far as shading and color use are concerned, I went from one extreme to the other. In the front part, behind the pins, is just a solid green. In the distant golf course, the mountains, and the sky, the color variations and gradations suggest three-dimensional space and texture.

The sky and the clouds are done in the most traditional way; depth is suggested in the clouds by using dark and medium dark lines, and leaving the clouds themselves white.

The mountains are done in violet, but with blue and red. Scattered stitches of other colors in some of

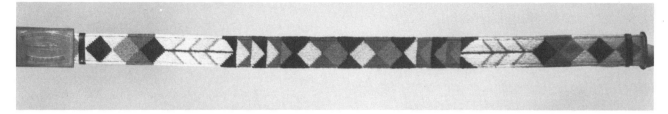

Photo 44. Wells Fargo Man's Belt.

Photo 45. Detail of Wells Fargo Man's Belt.

the solid areas suggest texture and depth. I did this to a great extent behind the golfer, by using various shades of blue, to make that area more interesting. This and the whiteness of the golfer's shirt help draw your eye to the golfer.

If the colors in the vest had all been handled in the same way (the Tent Stitch is used throughout) the design would have been visually boring if not outright confusing. To obtain visual clarity and interest, solid areas are contrasted with broken-up areas of color.

In the Adam and Eve Stool (Color Plates 1 and 2) I used the Tent Stitch on No. 18 mono canvas with 1-ply Persian yarn. Shading in the figures of Adam and Eve suggests the roundness of the human body.

Parts of the figure of Eve are shaded by using darkened tones of the flesh color, on the contours of the arms and breasts.

Right behind Eve, a light, a medium, and a dark tone of one color—blue—suggest the play of light in the atmosphere. I broke up the color to simulate the play of light on a surface. I used this as a foil or contrast against the light–dark modeling to achieve variety and interest.

To create variety from one part of the design to another, I put a solid, unbroken blue area behind Adam—to make his background different from Eve's background. Although the figures are modeled in a traditional light–dark shading technique, the tree trunk is a flat red. I also made the leaves flat. There is some shading in the apple and the snake.

Light–dark shading is used in the Adam and Eve Stool as a highlight. There is no law that says everything in your design has to be shaded throughout in the same way. I suggest you consider this approach:

Plate 43. Man's Golf Course Vest.

When you are using the Tent Stitch to paint a picture, think about contrasting in one design various ways of showing depth and texture. Use some flat areas, some modeled or shaded areas, some dotted areas—even some striped areas.

Shading is used in the Creation Panels (Photos 46, 47, and 48) not to show roundness of form, or even to indicate depth in nature. It is used just to enrich and enliven flat areas. I have tried to use the light–dark variation expressively, and to vary the amounts and types of shading to create a satisfying visual unity. In these panels, shading variation is coordinated with textural variation.

The sky behind the tree in the top panel is relatively more shaded than the earth, which does have a certain amount of light–dark shading. However, the sky is much more shaded than the tree trunk, which

is really not shaded at all and appears dense. This panel (Photo 48) illustrates how shading in one piece does not have to be done with the same amount of force or in the same intensity from part to part. Shading can be used to a greater and lesser extent from one part of a design to another to produce a cohesive unity. This is basically the same technique of balancing amounts and types of shading as in the Adam and Eve Stool, parts of which are highly shaded and other parts not shaded at all. In general, a design becomes more interesting as the shading is handled in a varying, contrasting, and balancing way.

You may have observed that you can see shading effects quite clearly in black-and-white photographs. It is often easier to see shading effects in black-and-white; because color is not present, it does not distract you from seeing light–dark contrasts.

Needlepoint is an excellent medium for shading. Stitches besides the Tent Stitch can be used for shading and figurative as well as nonfigurative designs can be shaded.

The Recent Burden Stitch (Fig. 71, page 91; Figs. 82a and 82b) is used as the background and dominating texture of the Creation Panels. They were done on No. 10 mono canvas with Persian yarn, tapestry wool, silk and linen. Each panel was worked on a floor frame.

The Recent Burden Stitch is a combination of Tramé and Brick Stitch and I have made the Brick Stitch go over 6 canvas threads. You could, of course, vary that number.

The Darkness Panel (Photo 46) is a good example of how you can allow a design to grow out of the structure of the stitch. All the shapes in the panel were found by imagining rectangular areas of Recent Burden Stitches, with smaller rectangular areas removed or subtracted, and then allowing each indentation and each protrusion to lock into each other. I tried to make each of the shapes different one from the other.

It is possible to be expressive in one's textural use, because the imaginative or poetic association of texture with symbol adds depth and meaning to the image.

Photo 48. Creation Panel: Earth, Tree and Sky.

Photo 47. Creation Panel: Sun, Moon and Stars.

Photo 46. Creation Panel: Darkness.

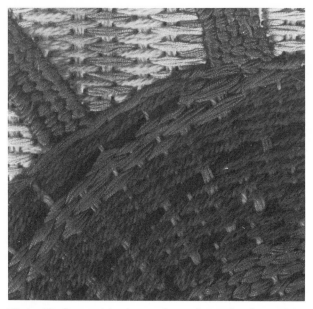

Photo 49. Sun and background; needleweaving is used for the sun and its rays.

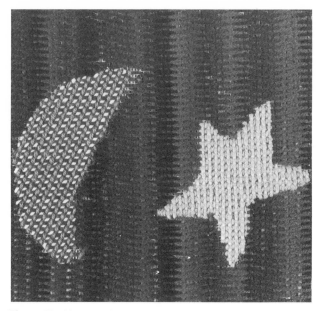

Photo 50. Moon and star.

Fig. 82a. The Recent Burden Stitch as used for the backgrounds shown in Photos 49, 50, and 53.

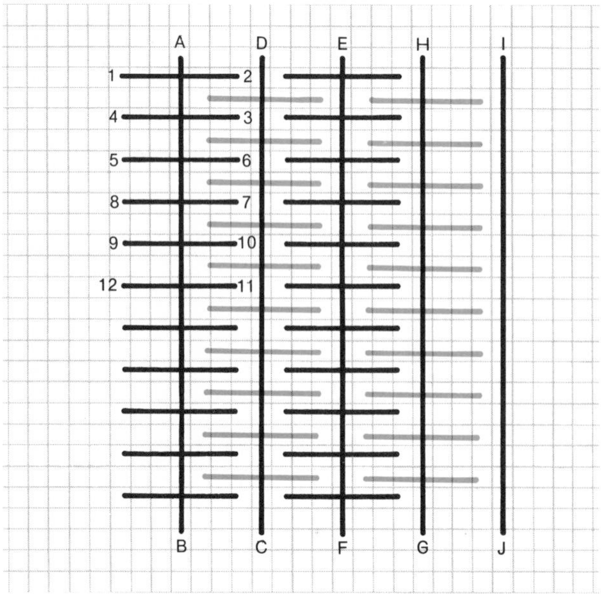

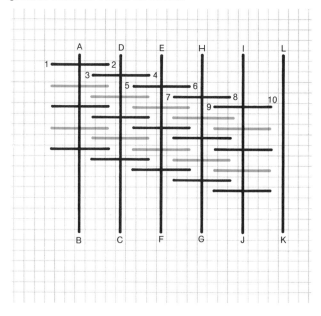

Fig. 82b. The Recent Burden Stitch as used for the backgrounds shown in Photos 51 and 52.

Photo 51. Tree.

Photo 53. Detail of Darkness Panel.

Photo 52. Bush.

Using the White of the Canvas for Texture and Color

Needlepoint canvas provides a unique and fascinating texture. In the Earth, Tree, and Sky Panel (Photo 48), the canvas is allowed to show through for design purposes. The Lattice Work Wall Hanging (Color Plate 44) makes use of the textural effect of bare canvas.

The latter piece started out as a practice canvas for a color version of Lattice Work. As I kept changing and working with my colors, the color effects of layers became fascinating. Instead of pulling out and discarding the colors that were displeasing, I left them there and just kept building on top of them, very much interested by the color and textural effects thus created. I built up some of the diamonds and left others with the canvas showing through. Even the white of the canvas was combined with the yarn colors to get the color I wanted. These sparser diamonds provide in the context of the design a sparkling texture, even though needlepoint canvas would not usually be described as sparkling.

Many stitches are suitable to this approach. Any stitch that involves Tramé, layers, or a substructure of Cross Stitching will work well.

Practicing the Color Contrasts

Had this Mini-Course in Color Fundamentals been given in person in my studio, I know I would have felt the need to explain in even greater detail why color contrasts are important, and how you can start practicing them.

You might have protested, "Why bother so much about contrasts? Isn't it better to choose according to similarity, and thereby achieve color harmony? Doesn't harmony mean a pleasing combination, nothing discordant? If we don't want discord, then why not leave out contrast and difference? The less contrast the better!"

In my view, using color contrast is essential to good design. Remember that when you put one color next to another each is saying: "Look at me! Enjoy me or my quality! Enjoy me more by seeing me in relation to another color that is similar or related yet different."

My firm belief is that color harmony is developed best by using contrasts and relationships—color variation—in one piece of work. Variation is, indeed, the key word here. In designing or working with visual elements, be they texture, color, space, or shape, we need first to be aware of or interested in total unity. Then we attempt to develop that unity, give it richness and meaning, by putting together contrasting effects, in this case contrasting color effects.

The same thing is true of color as is true of texture. The eye feeds on variety! The eye loves variety! Our eye gets bored and turns away if everything we are looking at seems too similar. As designers, we need to know how to harness variety to create a total visual unity.

Every visual design is made up of parts. Our aim is to make those parts clearly distinguishable from each other so that they are visible and interesting, and yet hold up their place in the total scheme. Here is where variation helps. The parts must also be related to each other, so that when we are finished we have one visual unity, not three or four. Although we want contrast, variety, and interest, we still don't wish a color, or any other element, to appear foreign to a design. If we put in too much difference or contrast, a design will fall apart. If we put in too little, the design will be dull and ineffectual and empty. Balance is essential.

I have tried in the Mini-Course to give you basic information so that you will practice with colors. Almost everybody will practice the stitches—how many of us will practice with colors?

The first and most important way is to look at colors and think about them. Think about them in terms of color contrasts.

Think about color when you have a spare moment, when you are waiting for your child at the dentist, when you are sitting in your car waiting for the light to change, or when you are looking at a decayed wall. You can start practicing by just looking at the colors

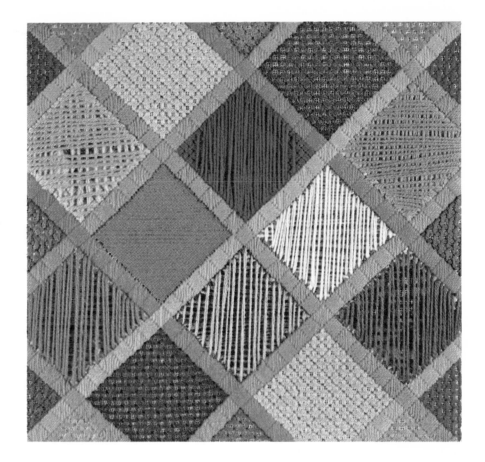

Plate 44. Lattice Work Wall Hanging.

of your clothes, the colors of your house, the colors of paintings.

We are lucky because the whole world is composed of color. If you wish to study or think about color, you don't have to go very far. One of the reasons I love color so much is that color is always here. No one is ever deserted by color. It is always something that surrounds me, and something to which I can react. Color can soothe me when I am angry, alone, or hurt.

Today, largely because of the advances of science, color is superabundant and almost, in my opinion, used to death. The overflow of color can create problems! There is much jangling and manipulation of nerves, emotions, and responses with color. Sometimes I think we are surrounded by more color than we know what to do with! Artists, designers, creative people in the visual field find themselves with a real

challenge: how to use color in a delicate, strong, fine, powerful, and, most important of all, personal and expressive way.

As you read, think about, absorb and practice the lessons of this Mini-Course, also look inward and study your own reactions to how colors are used.

Color can sing! It can glow! It can vibrate! Every color, and the way that it is used with others, has an effect on your eye and your heart. To use color in an expressive and emotional way, you must trust your own instinct, your own responses, and your own feelings. You have to use your own involvement because it is totally impossible to know how anybody else will respond. To me, color is the most subjective and most relative of the visual elements.

As you make thinking about color contrasts a part of your everyday life, and as you develop appreciation and enjoyment of them, you will come to use color contrasts in your needlepoint, just as you have learned to employ texture contrasts. Gradually you will learn to use color variation to construct a design.

Training yourself to think of color as an interacting, constantly changing force is bound to enrich your understanding and use of color. As I open my mind to color, and as I see more and more in color, naturally I am able to make more artistic use of what color has to offer. As much as I have practiced and learned about color, I am still fascinated by it, and always eager to try to understand somebody else's theory or point of view. The more that I understand colors, the more that I can see in them, the more I am able to feel them, enjoy them and use them.

When I select colors and work with them in a needlepoint piece, I discipline myself not to think of my color likes and dislikes. There are plenty of colors I don't wear, because I feel they do not become my complexion and coloring. But I try twice as hard not to neglect them in my designing, because I recognize my tendency to disregard them, to turn away from them. There are colors I would not use in my home, because of the emotional effect they may have on me when used in large pervasive quantities. I try twice as hard not to overlook those colors in my needlepoint work, because I know I need them despite a tendency to neglect them.

The great thing that needlepoint can do for you is to give you the opportunity to experiment with color. Needlepoint can give you the opportunity to question your old color habits and responses, and in doing so, you will find that you move into a deeper and richer, infinitely more rewarding emotional, expressive, and technical level.

If you wish to do your own color designing, remember that you are the designer. Do not belittle your own instincts, judgments, and feelings. Just try to expand them into areas that you might never have touched before. Try to use the contrasts of color as you continue to learn about them. Expanding and deepening your color concepts and usage will enable you to use needlepoint as an expressive art medium.

Another way to practice your colors, and thereby deepen your needlepoint color sense, is to do one or more of the designs offered in this book, as closely as possible to the colors shown.

By doing, or at least studying, these designs you will see that they are constructed on a simple repeat basis: repetition of rows, diagonal stripes, checkerboard alternation. Color is used to bring out and develop the repeat or nonrepeat design. At the same time, I try to use color as poetically and expressively as possible to construct a design.

As you study the color pieces in this book, when you handle and work with colors yourself, you will, first of all, see color contrasts and color fundamentals in action. As a result, you will be encouraged to branch out and become more experimental in your own color use. You will be encouraged to use the Mini-Course background, and even more important than that, you will just automatically get ideas. When you do your next design, you may start out with two or three colors that I used together, leaving out the others, and adding in some of your own selection.

You will start to work with color, perhaps at first following my lead, but then going off on your own. I am sure you will want to make your own color versions of the designs that have been pictured. And I hope that at some point, you will try to do everything yourself: the texture, the pattern, the image, the color—maybe even making up the stitch!

I also hope that you will enjoy feeling and responding to the colors in my designs. After all, what every artist dreams about is that somebody else will respond to and enjoy the colors and forms that he has put together, that he has found beautiful or interesting or expressive!

For further study of color, I recommend the following books, which form an important part of my color library among others listed in the Bibliography: *The Art of Color: The Subjective Experience and Objective Rationale of Color*, by Johannes Itten; *Basic Color, An Interpretation of the Ostwald Color System*, by Egbert Jacobson; and *Color: Basic Principles and New Directions* by Patricia Sloan.

THREE

Textured Needlepoint and Interior Design

GUIDELINES FOR YOUR USE

The Decorative Functions of Needlepoint

An important part of my work is to design needlepoint objects that will not only fit effectively into a client's interior decor but also contribute to, enhance, and help construct that interior.

In this respect, I become an interior designer specializing in needlepoint use. Almost all the designs shown were designed as commissions for clients to make and use. I have tried to create needlepoint textures, patterns, and objects that will serve useful and varying decorative and functional purposes. Their flexibility and adaptability are a source of gratification to me.

One great advantage of needlepoint is its decorative use. You can start with a simple, strong structure in your home, and gradually over the years you can fill it with important or incidental needlepoint pieces.

There are three ways in which needlepoint can be used in a decorative interior: (1) As a major furnishing, such as a large rug, risers for a staircase, a set of dining-room chair seats, a screen. (2) As an accessory —sofa and chair pillows, floor pillows, accent rugs or floor paintings, bench cushions. (3) As an art object— from a large wall hanging to a small piece set on a table easel.

The larger and more functional, decoratively speaking, the needlepoint object is, the more consideration should be given to the decorative demands of the room or home. In this way, you can use needlepoint to pull a room together and make it a decorative whole. A beautiful large needlepoint rug can establish a room. The Staircase (Color Plate 48) has an important decorative role. It is the very first feature that one sees upon entering the home. My client wisely decided to highlight it by keeping everything else in the front hall subdued and unpatterned, to get the full decorative impact of the staircase.

As the needlepoint object becomes more "accessoire" or auxiliary in nature, one has more freedom.

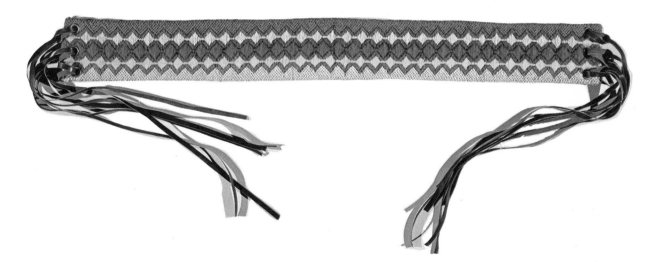

Plate 45. Belt with same stitch pattern as Wall Hanging for Lawyer's Office.

Accessories should play up or introduce certain colors in a room, and sofa pillows are very often just the place to put strong and striking accent colors or patterns.

But the needlepoint art object can be a world in itself; it does not have to be functional. More and more, people are thinking of their homes as backgrounds for art. If you think in terms of needlepoint art objects, you will continue to find additional decorative uses and places for them. Here, however, it is logical to give thought to where the object is to be placed. The Adam and Eve Wall Hanging (Color Plates 25, 29 through 36) was designed for a master bedroom done in blues and greens with orange accents.

The use of needlepoint in interior design is a very interesting subject; an entire book could be devoted to it alone. This chapter will only touch on some of my own attitudes, preferences, ground rules, and habits.

When I am thinking of the decorative use of my designs, I tend to think of them as three-dimensional fabrics that can be cut and used in whatever shapes, colors, and functions I wish.

I also keep in mind that an interior is not one visual space that is seen all at once. Most paintings and needlepoint designs are. An interior is rather more like a series of groupings or compositions, through which we move, carrying visual ideas, messages, and impressions from part to part.

Importance of the Character and Environment of the Home

When a client asks me to design a needlepoint object that will become part of the decorative interior, I ask many questions.

■ What type of room and home is it? Country, formal, cozy, dramatic?

■ Is the room and home contemporary in feeling, or is it furnished with antiques, and if so, what period? What are the structural details of the room? Are the floors patterned in any way?

■ What colors are used in the room and elsewhere in the home? What types of materials and textures?

I like my client to describe the room and home to

Plate 46. Detail of belt.

me. If I can, I visit the home. I make rather detailed notes, which I consult and think about before ever starting to design the piece. I am looking primarily for color and texture information in relation to the general atmosphere of the home. I consider the downstairs or the company rooms as a unity. The bedrooms or more private areas of the home are also parts of the total unity.

Having absorbed the atmosphere and general overall feeling, I concentrate on the details. Anything that I can learn about my client's home environment gives me very strong clues as to tastes and preferences. These are important because I believe the sine qua non of any interior and any needlepoint piece is that the person who makes it should like it!

The client is always asked to choose from my stock of wools the colors that are closest to the colors in the room being planned for, as well as adjacent rooms. And I always ask for as many samples as possible of the materials in them. I very much like to see samples of fabrics, materials, wallpapers, and other needlepoint pieces as well.

My primary interest, of course, is in the background fabric or material that the needlepoint will be on or will be seen next to. However, I also like to know the colors of the floors, walls, and even the colors of the flowers that the client likes to place in the room.

This preliminary thinking is extremely important. It is the foundation of wise decorating decisions. From this point on, the most important tools are the colors and materials used in the room.

Color Structures of Rooms

Rooms fall into various types of color structures:

1. No-color or neutral: When the basic scheme of a room is neutral, it is an artist's delight. One can utilize strong, vivid colors as decorative highlights. Highly intense or softer chromatic forms of the neutral colors can be used. Almost anything that appears in this type of room can take on an objet d'art feeling.

2. One-color or monochromatic: This type of color scheme can be enlivened, enriched, and broadened by using warms and cools of the one color. Thus a room that is built on light, medium and dark shades of red can also include pinks, oranges, and violets.

3. Two-color rooms: These could be blue and white, blue and yellow, black and white, or other combinations. In two-color rooms you can use complementary colors as accents. You can also use mixtures, tints, and shades of the two colors.

4. Multicolored rooms: These can be built on any range of colors from earth to primary. You could have a neutral, beige, as the dominant color, and use two strong colors with it—red and black. Three or more colors can be analogous, that is, one next to the other on the color wheel—blue, blue-green, green. Or they could be spaced around the color wheel, as the secondaries are—orange, green, and violet. More and more, multicolored rooms are being used as backgrounds for art objects.

Analyzing color information, I decide which color structure is closest to my client's. This gives me a color framework within which to work. Very often, the existing colors of the room do not quite fulfill the color structure. Then I make the needlepoint design for the room fulfill the structure to give the interior more decorative strength. The needlepoint may well pull the room together.

Coordinating Patterns, Textures, and the Environment

Within a structured color framework, I like to mix and contrast patterns and textures. I like very much to design pillows in pairs or threesomes.

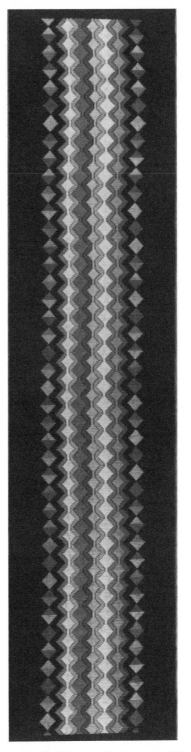

Photo 54. Wall Hanging for Lawyer's Office.

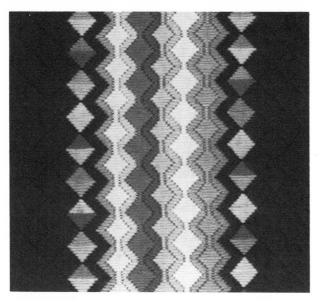

Photo 55. Detail of Wall Hanging for Lawyer's Office.

Fig. 83*. Basic stitch pattern used in Wall Hanging for Lawyer's Office (Photo 54) and Belt (Color Plates 45 and 46).

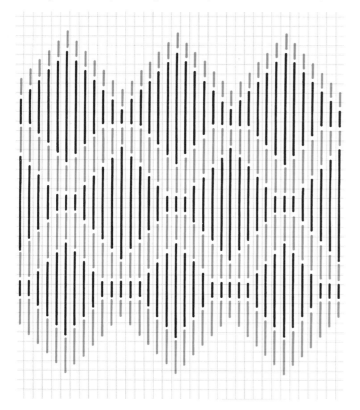

Coordinating patterns and textures is easily done by changing the scale from design to design, or from design to background fabric. Geometric can be put on geometric if there is a change in scale.

Patterns such as Patchwork I (Color Plates 3 and 5), Jacob's Ladder (Color Plate 8), and Lattice Work (Color Plates 9, 10, and 38) work very well with floral prints, whether large or small scaled. The angular and architectural nature of the geometric abstract designs contrasts well with the fluidity of the florals. Conservative as well as innovative decorators agree that geometrics work well with florals.

Color can unite and coordinate patterns and textures in a room. *See* Using Color Contrasts to Create the Pattern and Coordinate Two Pillows (pages 34–35).

Patterns and textures can be related by motif.[28] If you are fortunate enough to own an Oriental rug, take one of its motifs, enlarge it, and work it boldly in striking strong colors. You will be relating the needlepoint design to the rug, but you will not be repeating the rug. There is an interesting dimensionality of time in having a beautiful old piece of weaving on your floor and making a design in a contemporary idiom that relates to it.

Lattice Work, Variation 2 (Color Plate 38) and Mysterious Islands (Color Plate 28) make a beautiful combination on a beige sofa. In this room, there is a lovely soft blue Persian rug on the floor. The mandala that is in the center of Lattice Work relates to the design of the rug. Incidentally, these two pillows were not designed expressly for this home; they had been created for two other settings. The designs just work beautifully together here.

This idea of dimensionality of time is an important one to me. I like to use traditional and old needlework with new and contemporary needlework. One of my Mountain Peaks designs (Color Plates 13 and 16) could be used effectively with a traditional bargello design.

I love to watch the needlepoint objects in my home mellow with time. The gradual softening of color is beautiful to see, and that adds another time dimension.

I like to think of numerous ways to group and

overlap needlepoint pieces. I extend the idea of using texture on texture and pattern on pattern to using needlepoint piece on needlepoint piece. I like to use needlepoint textures in relation to wood, velvet, leather, and glass textures.

Conversational areas or groupings of furniture are good places to utilize textural contrast, and where you can use needlepoint very well. The textural interest in your needlepoint pillows will greatly increase the interest of pieces of furniture that are placed close together.[29] You can create a conversational or reading area by designing a needlepoint ottoman to join together two chairs.[30]

As you look carefully at the materials, textures and details in your home, you will start to analyze. This in itself will give you good design starting points. You will be able to pick up a motif or idea from a fabric or wallpaper and elaborate on that.

The Staircase (Color Plate 48) was developed by using as a starting point the material that covers two of the sofas in a client's living room. The sofa material is a woven floral pattern. A lovely lineny type of material, it conveys a strong feeling of weaving linked with embroidery. Using several of its qualities—a flower motif, a woven and embroidered surface, plus the linen feeling—I created the Staircase design. The

Plate 47. Night Garden Headboard.

Greg Molesworth

SELVAGE

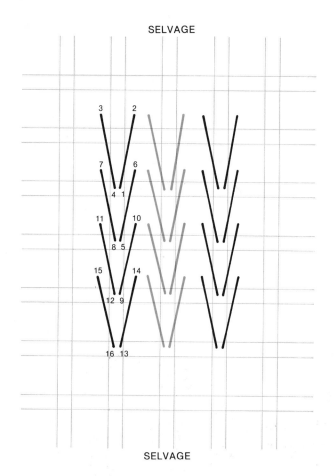

SELVAGE

Fig. 84. Soumak Stitch on double-mesh rug canvas.

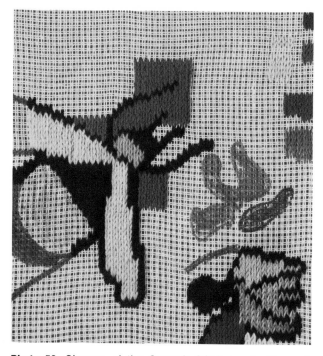

Photo 56. Closeup of the Soumak Stitch on double-mesh rug canvas.

Renaissance Stitch is used because it conveys a feeling of weaving and helps to make the pattern stand out from the Tent Stitch background. Linen as well as Persian yarn was used.

If you use wallpaper in your room, consider that as one of your materials and patterns. Rather than copy the wallpaper, pick out and use one visual theme from it. Elaborate on that motif and try to make it into an expressive unity.

This is what I did when I designed the Night Garden Headboard (Color Plate 47) for a girl's room. My client brought me the materials—the bedspread and wallpaper. Originally, she had thought that she wanted to repeat the wallpaper pattern on the head-

board. However, I felt strongly that it would be more interesting visually to take just the idea of one tulip and put it into a somewhat different shape. I wanted to make the tulip convey an embracing feeling of protecting the child when she goes to sleep at night. And because it's nighttime, I conceived the idea of making it a night garden rather than a day garden, and therefore used a dark blue background, which in addition would be practical and long-wearing. I put a butterfly and bee in because those do go with flowers and belong in a garden. The headboard is most effective and the child loves it, and that, of course, makes me very happy. The Night Garden Headboard was done with the Soumak Stitch on No. 5/10 double-mesh rug canvas with Persian yarn and linen (Fig. 84 and Photo 56). When doing the Soumak Stitch keep the selvage edges to top and bottom.

Part of the fun of finding designs in books is imagining how they will look as objects in your home, as they are shown, or in other shapes, forms, colors, and functions.

When you make needlepoint for your home, you are bound to get into making decorating decisions, and that is good. This is one of the many ways that needlepoint can help you to exercise your own creativity.

Think of the designs offered as three-dimensional fabrics or textiles. Use the Interior Design Guidelines that follow to help you choose which designs you want to use, and to help you know how to use them imaginatively and with good taste. As you think in interior design terms, you will then be able to adapt the design to serve your interior's particular needs.

Use the Mini-Course in Color Fundamentals and the information in this section. Work within the en-vironment's structure, but create it and add to it at the same time. Do not be overly hindered by it and do not simply repeat what you find there.

The environment is important. I try to work within it, but I also try to do something different that will still relate. I want my needlepoint design to show up and be noticed. A piece of needlepoint can be like an art object, a world in itself, that will draw you to it, and affect you in a compelling way.

Allow yourself to be ruled primarily by your own instinct, taste, and judgment. After all, if you are interested enough to make objects for your home, you are bound to have an artist's soul somewhere deep inside you!

Summary of Interior Design Guidelines

1. Study the room. Decide what color structure (*see* page 133) it is closest to or which one you would like it to be. Use the needlepoint that you put into the room to fulfill the color structure.

2. You can achieve tremendous variety with any group of colors, no matter how limited, by lightening and darkening, warming or cooling them, and making them more or less intense.

■ Apply what you have learned about color chords in your interior designing as well as in needlepoint. Refer to the Mini-Course in Color Fundamentals if necessary.

3. You can alter the expressive feeling and mood of a needlepoint piece very easily by changing its colors, the type of thread it is done with, and the size mesh canvas.

4. Do not be afraid of mixing and contrasting pattern with pattern and texture with texture. In doing this, you are following nature's habit of mixing patterns and textures. Just think for a moment about tree trunks and leaves, pine cones and needles, sand and shells.

■ Link different scaled patterns together by relating their colors.

■ Pick up, repeat, and elaborate on a motif.

5. The materials of needlepoint provide the perfect means to change the scale of any design, simply by changing the size mesh canvas that is used.

6. Since we are always working on squared canvas with stitches, the patterns that are developed are going to have similar or related motifs, almost automatically. You can capitalize on these relationships: Squares, diamonds, rectangles, diagonals, horizontals, and verticals seem to grow most naturally out of needlepoint canvas. And these are, incidentally, the same types of patterns that develop in woven materials.

Plate 48. Staircase.

138

Staircase

Step-by-Step Directions

[*Color Plate 48*]

MATERIALS:

No. 12 mono canvas (from a 54-inch wide roll, if possible)
Persian yarn
Linen

DIMENSIONS:

The dimensions depend upon your own staircase. How to handle them will be discussed below.

STITCHES	ILLUSTRATIONS
Renaissance Stitch	Fig. 73
Smyrna Cross Stitch	Fig. 92
Tent Stitch	Figs. 5a, 5b, 5c, 5d, 5e

Work from Color Plate 48 and from Chart 4. (Chart 4 gives riser 3 with color specifications slightly simpler than those shown in Color Plate 48.) Only the risers are done in needlepoint; the treads are covered with carpeting. A smooth, nontweedy carpeting works well with this design.

Step 1

Measure carefully each riser of your staircase. Keep a written record of the dimensions.

■ Add at least 8 inches to both the height and width of the risers before you cut the canvas. This will give you a 4-inch-wide margin around the actual dimensions. Although the necessary mounting seam allowance is narrow, in a project as big as this, where precision is extremely important, you may make an error, which you can correct if you have left yourself a sufficient canvas margin.

Step 2

Cut out of canvas each riser with the wide margin added to the dimensions.

■ Bind each riser with wide white bias tape.
■ Mark the dimensions of each riser on the canvas with a light-gray permanent marking pen.
■ Depending upon the type of staircase, decide where the center line of each riser must be. *Do not do this until you have read Step 3.*

Color Numbers and Amounts Needed
Staircase (For six risers, as shown in Chart 4.)
Persian Yarn

Color	Approximate Amount	Colbert 6	Paterna
Warm white (background)	2 pounds	100	026
Very deep rust	2 ounces	61	210
Medium rust	1 ounce	63	255
Light red	2 ounces	13	852
Deep yellow-green	1 ounce	90	545
Deep green	1 ounce	2	510
Deep yellow ochre	1 ounce	43	433
Very deep leaf green	1 ounce	102	505

Fawcett Linen

Color	Size	Approximate Amount
Black	10/5	4 packages
Avocado	10/5	5 packages
Spanish gold	10/5	2 packages
Yellow	10/5	2 packages
Orange	10/5	2 packages
Chartreuse	10/2	2 packages
Dark green	10/5	2 packages
Gold	10/5	1 package

RISER 1

RISER 2

RISER 3

RISER 4

RISER 5

Chart 4. Color Key for Staircase Risers

Persian Yarn Colors

1 = Warm white (background of all the risers)
2 = Very deep rust
3 = Medium rust
4 = Light red

5 = Deep yellow-green
6 = Deep green
7 = Deep yellow ochre
8 = Very deep leaf green

Linen Colors

A = Black
B = Avocado
C = Spanish gold
D = Yellow

E = Orange
F = Chartreuse
G = Dark green
H = Gold

RISER 6

Step 3

How to decide where the center line of each riser must be

- Look carefully at Chart 4 and Color Plate 48. The broken lines in Chart 4 show the invisible center line that you must use when mounting the risers so that the total image matches up precisely.

- Mark this center line on each of your canvas risers, but it is important to note that the center line may not always be in the actual center of each canvas riser.

- If the risers of your staircase are all the same width, just use the center line of each canvas riser for the center line on Chart 4.

- However, if the risers vary, as the ones shown in Color Plate 48 or in some other way, analyze exactly how the design is constructed and works visually, so that you can work out the center line for yourself according to your own staircase needs.

- The center line—shown by the broken lines in Chart 4—*must* be in a straight vertical plumb line on your staircase, no matter what the dimensions of each riser may be.

- In the staircase shown in Color Plate 48, this center line is always the same distance from the left side of the staircase—or from the left side of each of the canvas risers. The distance of the center line from the right-hand side of some of the risers varies because the lower risers are wider than the top seven risers. Before going ahead with this project, be sure that you understand this concept.

Step 4

Having decided where the center line of each riser should be, mark it with a basting thread. Baste it so that you can pull the thread out of the riser when you start to do the background stitching. But stitch or mark the center line on the margin permanently so that the mounter will be able to see this center line clearly. The mounter will match up each riser according to that center line.

- To repeat: The center lines are shown in Chart 4 by the broken black lines.

- I prefer to mark the center lines with thread because even the lightest-gray marking pen or paint may show through the white background.

Step 5

Transfer the drawing of each riser from Chart 4.

- You can draw freehand with permanent marking pens or permanent paint.

- If you do not feel able to copy these drawings, have them enlarged by photostating them to the dimensions you need for your staircase. Use the dimensions of your narrowest riser as the dimensions of the photostat.[31] Then trace over the photostatic enlargement, putting each canvas riser directly over the enlargement and tracing directly onto the canvas.

- You need to photostat only risers 1, 2, 3, 4, and 5 as riser 6 is the same as riser 2.

- Notice that the direction of the large leaves in riser 4 (counting from the top) is reversed for riser 8. (*See also* Color Plate 48.) It is not necessary to do this, but it adds a touch of imperfection or of breaking the pattern that I like.

Step 6

Stitching the Risers

- Work from Chart 4 to follow the color, type of yarn, and stitch pattern.

- The floral design is done almost entirely in the Renaissance Stitch. Use 3-ply Persian yarn, 10/5 linen just as it comes, and 10/2 linen doubled.

- Fig. 73 (page 97) shows the Renaissance Stitch. The straight red lines in Chart 4 indicate the direction of the Tramé and therefore of the Renaissance Stitch for each of the parts.

- The black dots on the large leaves are done with Smyrna Cross Stitches (Fig. 92, page 151). Use 10/5 linen just as it comes. Each Smyrna Cross Stitch is indicated by a red star in Chart 4.

- Work the background of each riser in the Tent Stitch: Use 2-ply Persian yarn. Be sure to work the Tent Stitch keeping the selvages to your left and right.

- Remember to add on a few rows of Tent Stitching for the mounter's seam allowance.

Step 7

When you have finished the risers, have them blocked professionally by an upholsterer, an art store, or a carpet installer who knows how to block needlepoint.

■ Be sure to provide the blocker with the exact dimensions of your risers, telling him that you have added on a few rows for seam allowance, so that he will block the risers correctly to fit your staircase.

■ The carpet man will install the risers by nailing them to your staircase and by turning in the slight seam allowance you have allowed. He then will install the carpet for the treads.

■ A beautiful, neat, and precise job can be done by a professional carpet layer. He is well worth his hire, and I suggest that you do not try to install the staircase yourself. You will have put in hours of beautiful personal work and you should value it enough to have it finished just right.

Colors and Yarns Used in the Staircase

In the table that precedes, the approximate amount is for six risers as shown in Chart 4, each riser being 40 inches x 5½ inches. The exact amounts that you will need will depend upon the dimensions of your staircase and the number of risers that you make. Keep in mind that you do not even need a full staircase to use this design. You could take part of it and cover two steps or four steps. You could even make it work for three steps.

When buying the Persian yarn for this design make sure that you buy more than enough for the background color. Otherwise, if you have to go back for additional background yarn, you may find that the dye lot available is slightly different. The store where you buy your materials will help you to figure out how much you need in the beginning.

Also, it is not necessary to use linen for the staircase. If you prefer, the whole design can be done in Persian yarn.

Fawcett linen is obtainable packaged in 30-yard skeins (10/5) and in 45-yard skeins (10/2). You can order directly from Frederick J. Fawcett, Inc., 129 South Street, Boston, Massachusetts 02111.

Adapting the Staircase Design to Your Own Needs

The background color of the risers is indeed a fragile one, but I chose it because it works so well from an interior design point of view in the home for which it was planned. My client's husband made lucite covers for the risers which are kept on during the week and removed on weekends and when the family entertains. In addition, the children are grown, so this color scheme is not impractical in this home. If you have young children, do not choose a color scheme such as this.

If You Want to Change the Colors

Take the same basic idea, use the outline drawings, but adjust the colors to your own decorative and functional needs. Be sure to consider the color of the carpeting that you will use for the treads when you are constructing the color scheme of the entire design. If possible, obtain a sample of the carpeting that you will use. Above all, do not do the risers and then search around for the right color carpet. Consider the decorative and functional needs of your home as you are designing your own color scheme.

This is a challenging artistic design project, and I strongly recommend that you experiment with colored paper, paint, and practice studies before cutting any canvas for the finished work. When I did this design, I painted on paper the design of each of the risers, and tacked each paper riser in place on the actual staircase to make sure that the whole design worked. I also made some practice studies on canvas. This is indeed a designing project for an advanced, committed, and patient needleworker.

If You Cannot Obtain No. 12 Mono Canvas 54 inches Wide

Most staircase risers are about 40 inches wide so that if you use canvas 54 inches wide you can cut the risers perpendicular to the selvage edges. If you are unable to obtain No. 12 mono canvas 54 inches wide, use

36-inch-wide canvas. Simply cut the riser strips parallel to the selvage edges. Then be sure to do the background Tent Stitching while holding the selvage edges to your left and right. If you look closely at Color Plate 48, you will observe that this is exactly how this staircase was done.

Changing the Mesh of the Canvas

You can use a No. 14 canvas, or even finer if you wish, for this design, but I do not recommend a canvas any coarser than No. 12. In other words, do not use No. 10 canvas. The space you have to work with on a riser is very limited and the scale that you would achieve with a No. 10 canvas would not, in my opinion, work out well. If you decide to use a finer mesh canvas, remember (1) it will take you longer to complete the project and (2) you will have to experiment and work out for yourself the ply needed for the Persian yarn as well as the size needed for the Fawcett linen. Even if you use a No. 12 canvas you may have to adjust the ply and size of the materials, as indicated in paragraph 5 of the *Notes Applicable to All Step-by-Step Directions* (page xix).

FOUR

Designing Your Own Textured Needlepoint

The two projects offered in this section will help you develop a free and experimental approach to textured needlepoint designing. Along with the Summary of Design Principles, given at the end of the section, these two projects will help you to review and reinforce the ideas discussed throughout the book.

Plate 49. Patchwork II.

Project I

Wall Hanging Sampler of Selected Stitches

PURPOSE:

To acquaint yourself with some of the stitches that are appropriate for creating textured needlepoint.

MATERIALS:

No. 3 mono rug canvas
Rug wool
Persian yarn
Other embroidery threads

SUGGESTED STITCHES	ILLUSTRATIONS
These stitches work well in rug wool on No. 3 mono rug canvas:	
Cross	Figs. 85a, 85b
Herringbone	Fig. 86
Herringbone and Cross	Fig. 87
Two-color Herringbone	Fig. 88
Rice	Fig. 89
Double	Fig. 90
Knotted	Fig. 91
Smyrna Cross	Fig. 92
Interlocking Gobelin	Fig. 93
Web	Fig. 94
Kalem	Fig. 95
Darning	Fig. 79a
Double Leviathan	Fig. 4a–e
Chain	Fig. 63

Procedure

Play with the stitches until you understand how they are constructed. Don't even worry about designing for total effect. Just have fun, follow your instincts, and try to learn something about each stitch.

Only one hint about the total design is necessary: Start work in the middle of the canvas—not in a corner or at the edge.

Note how the appearance of a stitch changes when you do it with rug wool and with Persian yarn. See what happens when you vary the number of canvas threads a stitch crosses. Try to develop each stitch in terms of the three stitch variables: size, direction, and movement (*see* pages 58–60). You will soon find patterns and design ideas emerging from your experimentation.

The advantages of using rug wool and rug canvas for this project are that the work goes fast and you can see what you are doing. It is not necessary to use a frame because the rug canvas is extremely firm. Also you can make changes easily.

I did the Wall Hanging Sampler shown in Photo 57, when I first started using various stitches in needlepoint. The charcoal color of the background done in the Interlocking Gobelin Stitch highlights the stitch patterns. The wall hanging is mounted on plywood.

Ideas for several designs evolved from this piece, among them Patchwork II, Afterglow, and a Herringbone and Cross Stitch Eyeglass Case.

Patchwork II (Color Plate **49**) is made with rug wool and Persian yarn on No. 3 mono rug canvas (Photo 58) using the Herringbone (Fig. 86), Rice (Fig. 89), Kalem (Fig. 95), and Cross Stitches (Figs. 85a and 85b). The Afterglow design is used for both a pillow (Photo 59) and a tote bag (Photo 60). The Herringbone, Rice, Kalem, and Cross Stitches are used in rug wool on No. 3 mono rug canvas. The Eyeglass Case and its stitch pattern are shown in Photos 61 and 62.

Photo 57. Wall Hanging Sampler.

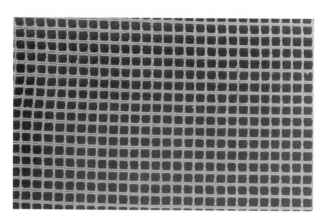

Photo 58. No. 3 mono rug canvas.

Photo 60. Afterglow used for tote bag.

Photo 59. Afterglow used for pillow.

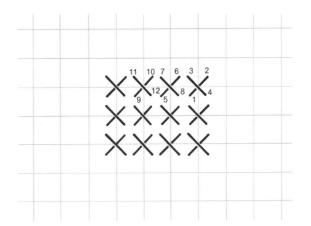

Fig. 85a. The Cross Stitch: Do each stitch all at once.

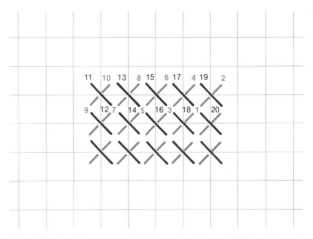

Fig. 85b. Another way of doing the Cross Stitch: Do one layer at a time.

Fig. 86. The Herringbone Stitch.

Photo 61. Herringbone and Cross Stitch Eyeglass Case, worked on No. 3 mono rug canvas with rug wool.

Photo 62. Herringbone and Cross Stitch on No. 3 mono rug canvas with rug wool.

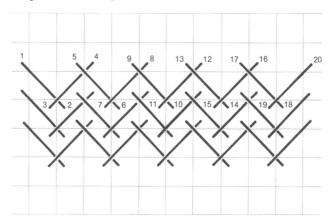

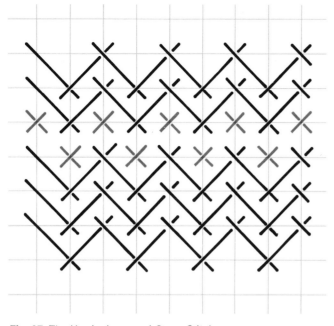

Fig. 87. The Herringbone and Cross Stitch.

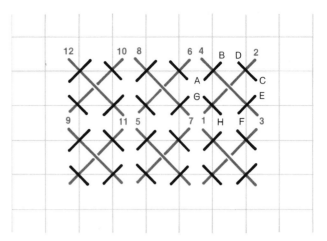

Fig. 89. The Rice Stitch. Use 6-ply Persian yarn for tie-down corner stitches.

Fig. 88. The two-color Herringbone Stitch. Do bottom layer in one color, top in another. Back Stitch between rows of Herringbone Stitch.

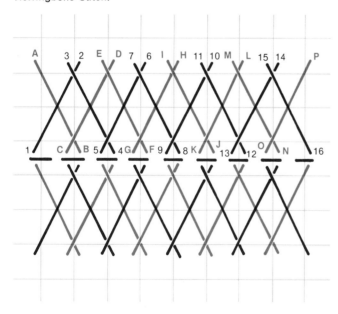

Fig. 90. The Double Stitch. Do large crosses in one color, small crosses in another.

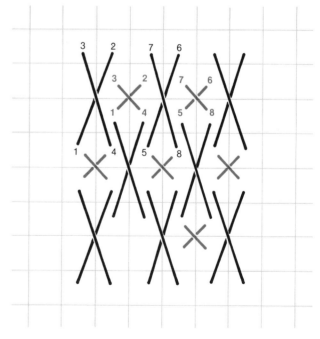

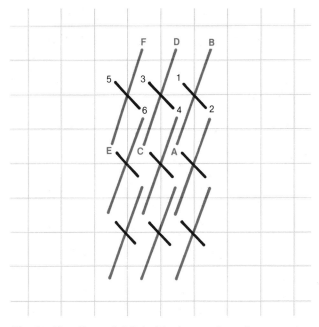

Fig. 91. The Knotted Stitch. Try bottom layer in one color, tie-down stitches in another.

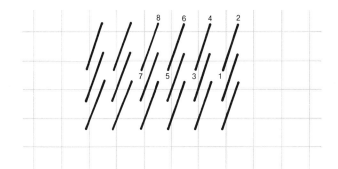

Fig. 93. The Interlocking Gobelin Stitch.

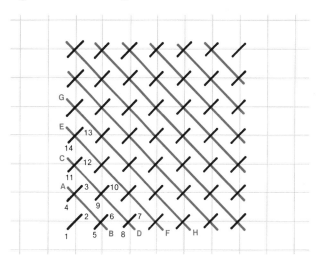

Fig. 94. The Web Stitch. Do Tramé in one color, tie-down stitches in another. Chain Stitch around Web Stitch squares.

Fig. 95. The Kalem Stitch. Work from top to bottom. For each row, turn canvas and start down again.

Fig. 92. The Smyrna Cross Stitch.

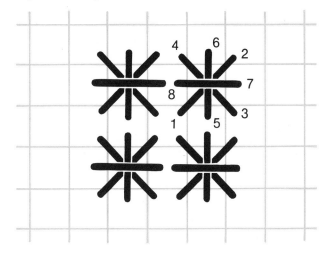

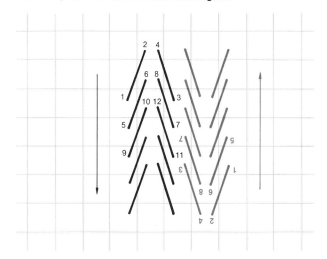

Fewer Stitches Rather Than More

If you are about to embark on your first do-it-yourself designing project, consider starting with one stitch alone. From here on, you will find it easy to add more stitches, always keeping in mind that the wise designer limits the number of different stitches in a single design. Allow your imagination to develop each stitch to its full potential.

For example, Instant Bargello (Color Plate 50) shows that a broad range of colors can be used when doing just the Herringbone Stitch (Fig. 86) on No. 3 mono rug canvas with rug wool.

Spectrum II (Color Plate 51) is done in just one stitch—Cross Stitch (Figs. 85a and 85b)—on either No. 3 mono or No. 6 (3/6) double-mesh rug canvas, using rug wool. It is fun to do the underneath part of the Cross Stitch in one color and the top part in another. You can achieve a unique two-layered shading effect with very simple means.

The Herringbone Stitch (Fig. 86) and Cross Stitch (Figs. 85a and 85b) work well together (Fig. 87) and produce an interesting texture on No. 3 mono rug canvas with rug wool (Photo 62). The Eyeglass Case of Photo 61 is worked in this way.

Interpretation of a Child's Drawing

Visual variety can be created when using one stitch alone by changing the size of the stitch and by using several types of threads.

The Football Players (Color Plate 52 and Photo 63) is done on No. 24 (12/24) double-mesh canvas with the Tent Stitch. The figures are in silk, using the canvas 24 holes to the inch. Persian yarn is used for the background, using the canvas 12 holes to the inch. Two shades of green are used for the background to create a soft, tweedy texture that contrasts, yet relates to the smooth, silky texture of the figures. The Football Players is based on my 9-year-old son's drawing of Joe Kapp and Bubba Smith (Photo 64); that is why it is signed MW/DW.

Plate 50. Instant Bargello.

Plate 51. Spectrum II.

Photo 63. Detail of the Football Players.

Photo 64. David's drawing of Joe Kapp and Bubba Smith.

Plate 52. The Football Players.

Photo 65. Robin's Sampler.

Photo 66. Detail of Robin's Sampler: the Upright Cross Stitch over 6 canvas threads.

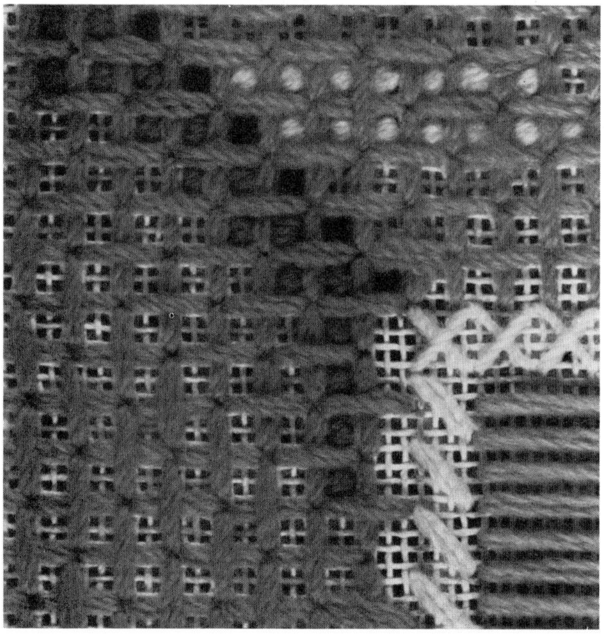

Photo 67. Detail of Robin's Sampler: the polka-dot corner is completed by filling in with the Cross Stitch.

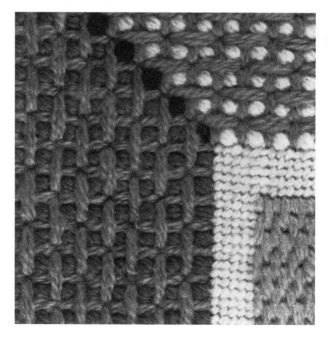

Project II

A Figurative Design Based on Objects, People, or a Scene

PURPOSE:

To help you develop confidence in your own drawing ability. You will soon realize that your own drawing ability will serve you perfectly well in the medium of needlepoint.

MATERIALS:

No. 10 or No. 12 mono canvas
Persian yarn
Tapestry wool
Embroidery linens and cottons

STITCHES

Use stitches that you are most familiar and comfortable with.

Procedure

Start out with a simple structure, with geometric shapes and forms symbolizing what you see in nature. For example, each of the images in Robin's Sampler (Photo 65) stands for something of importance to Robin Winter. Keep in mind that you will make your design simple in outline, enriching it in material and detail. (*See* Simplify and Symbolize, following.)

When composing your image, remember that the edges of the canvas play an important visual role in your design by creating background or negative space. In other words, think not only about the shape you draw onto the canvas, but also about the background shapes that are formed. Design considerations when drawing are summarized on page 156.

Choose your colors by constructing a color chord and orchestrating it. Refer if necessary to the Mini-course in Color Fundamentals (pages 107–128).

Try to create varying textures by utilizing what you have learned about texture contrasts. Ask yourself: What will be my dominant texture? What texture or textures will I use to accent or bring out the dominant one?

Ask yourself the same questions about color. Keep in mind that shading and color variation can be integrated with textural variation.

Think of what you are doing as collage or appliqué: putting together different textured materials to create a unity. Use cut-out pieces of textured materials— carpeting, upholstery, or dressmaking scraps—to help you visualize your idea. Or make a bold and quick study of your idea on practice canvas.

Simplify and Symbolize

I believe that one could happily spend a lifetime experimenting with stitches and creating patterns and textures based on those stitches—from the stitch point of view. I believe that one would get a tremendous amount of enjoyment out of it, without ever having to draw a face, a tree, or anything else. The vocabulary of stitches available in needlepoint permits creating and designing attractive, good-looking objects without ever having to draw anything to look like something else.

However, it would be unfortunate and unnecessary if you limited your experimentation in needlepoint design to that. A clumsily drawn face, dog, cat, or tree—as long as it's yours, as long as you are trying to express something—will turn out well. You'll do a good job, and you'll have lots of fun.

When working from realistic images, all you have to do is to simplify them in terms of a geometric or stylized shape, which as a result becomes a symbol.

In the Sun, Moon, and Stars Panel (Photo 47, page 123), I made the sun a half-hemisphere, with narrow rectangles for the rays. When symbolizing visual realities, I use the simplest possible geometric shapes that still retain character and significance. For instance, a doctor who saw the Adam and Eve Wall Hanging (Color Plate 29) asked me if I realized that the tree looks just like the female reproductive system? This hadn't entered my mind at all, but I was delighted that the form for the tree had something to do with birth.

Simplification of form is structurally necessary in needlepoint, especially when using textures and stitches, because then the textures can really be shown off. As you find simple shapes, you will be able to coordinate interesting textures. It was easy, for instance, to needleweave the sun, because the shape is a simple one. I just set up the armature for the needle-weaving with large buttonhole stitches following the half-hemisphere form. You can do this sort of thing too. Simplify a tree in terms of its trunk, branches, and leaves, and then by using stitchery and textures, you can create visual variation.

The Creation Panels (Photos 46, 47, and 48) show how natural phenomena can be stylized into shapes for needlepoint. Texture and shading create the particular feeling and expressiveness of each panel.

Design Considerations When Drawing

1. Proportion and Contrast

- Try to have a variety of shapes throughout your composition, rather than repeating a lot of similar shapes and sizes.

2. Positive Space and Negative Space

- The positive space is the shape that you draw onto the canvas. For example, in Fig. 96, the positive space is the sun, shown in white.
- The negative space is the background shape that is formed around the positive space; in Fig. 96, it is the black background shape around the sun.
- Considering the shape of negative space will help you to draw interesting positive shapes.
- To help yourself see the negative space as an important design element—rather than just background

—look at your work upside down and sideways. Turn the piece around in your hand, or else put it down on the floor and walk around it.

3. Separation and Overlapping of Shapes

- You can put your symbols, that is, the stylized shapes, out on the canvas, one by one, never allowing one to touch the other. This is what was done in the Adam and Eve Wall Hanging (Color Plate 29).
- You can also overlap shapes to create a feeling of depth. (See Fig. 97.)

Summary of Needlepoint Design Guidelines

1. Needlepoint is a textile art form in which texture is essential. Remember: You are constructing a three-dimensional fabric.

2. Needlepoint is an esthetic medium. It is suitable for nonfunctional art objects as well as functional ones.

3. Designing your own needlepoint is easier and more fun when you work from the stitch point of view than when you rely solely on illusionistic methods. Nevertheless, use fewer stitches rather than more.

4. Be willing to make changes as you go along. The willingness to change and adapt, combined with keeping your mind on the whole structure, is the secret of successful needlepoint designing.

5. Aim for variety, relationships, and contrasts within a unity.

- By choosing your limitations, you can create a structured framework. Within that, use contrasting textures, colors, shapes, and patterns.
- Structure your design so that it is clearly evident what dominates.
- Remember basic contrasts in stitch as well as color use: hard against soft, dark against light, high against low, shiny against matt, rough against smooth, opaque against transparent.

6. Use the structure and function of each stitch. Enhance and develop the stitch through pattern,

Fig. 96. Positive and negative space.

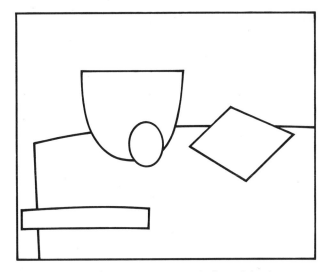

Fig. 97. Overlapping shapes create a feeling of depth.

composition, color, and types of yarn. Try to think of a stitch in terms of its armature.

7. Patterns are developed by repetition, emphasis or accent, and change.

■ Consider breaking the pattern.

■ Use imagination and free association to build a simple repeat pattern into a more complex visual organization.

8. Color use relates to textural use. The more textural variation is present in the design, the less color is needed for variation of surface, and the more simplified the color use can be.

■ Remember this rule: In general, the fewer the stitches used, the more color variation is needed. The greater the variety of stitches used, the fewer colors are needed.

■ Reflection and absorption of light by textured surfaces cause a certain amount of color variation even in a monochromatic textured surface. Therefore, try to combine or use different stitches so that you get different reflections and absorptions of light.

■ Finally, the use of color variation does, to a certain extent, block out the textural differences that you will perceive. Related to this is the fact that there is a textural feeling in color variation itself, because of the role that light plays when it hits a surface.

9. Color is the most subjective of the visual elements. It can be deeply expressive of emotion and feeling.

■ Choose one color chord and orchestrate it. Be sure it is clear what color dominates.

10. Use color contrasts.

■ Try to see and feel color as weight.

■ Contrast and use colors in terms of warmth and coolness, lightness and darkness, intensity and dullness, large and small amounts.

11. When coordinating designs, change the scale of each pattern. Repeat motifs and unite them with color.

12. Visually say what you mean and mean it. Exercise restraint.

13. Construct your design so that it is simple in outline, rich in material and detail.

14. Above all, please yourself and have fun!

Appendixes

Supplies and Mounting

Needlepoint supplies can be obtained in many stores throughout the country. For retail stores, see the Directory of Needlework Shops, which begins on page 162.

Wholesale Suppliers

Fawcett linen can be obtained on a retail and wholesale basis from:

Frederick J. Fawcett Inc.
129 South Street
Boston, Massachusetts 02111

Wood products, such as luggage racks, footstools, and serving trays, can be obtained on a retail and wholesale basis from:

Sudberry House
Wesley Avenue
Westbrook, Connecticut 06498

Colbert 6, Laine Colbert au Bon Pasteur, Soie d'Alger, and needlepoint canvas can be obtained on a wholesale basis from:

Handwork Tapestries Inc.
240 Lambert Avenue
Copiague, New York 11726

Paterna Persian yarn, Pat-Rug yarn and needlepoint canvas can be obtained on a wholesale basis from:

Paternayan Brothers, Inc.
312 East 95 Street
New York, New York 10028

Mounting, Commercial

Mounting of belts, telephone book covers, tennis racquet covers, pocketbooks, and many other types of needlepoint objects is done by:

Modern Needlepoint Mounting Company
11 West 32 Street
New York, New York 10001

Blocking and Mounting Techniques

I recommend that blocking and mounting be done professionally, either by your upholsterer, your art store, or by the mounter who specializes in a particular object. You can also, in most cases, take your pieces to the needlepoint store where you bought your materials. In view of the hours of work involved in creating your needlework and the many years of use and satisfaction derived, the cost of blocking and mounting is not great.

Of course, many people like to have the satisfaction of doing the entire piece, from beginning to end, and if you are one of those your motivation will help you to do a good job. Here are basic directions for blocking and mounting pillows and wall hangings.

Blocking

1. *Always* use *rustproof* tacks.
2. Cover a wooden board that is larger than the canvas with a piece of brown paper. Tack the paper down.
3. Refer to the dimensions of the design. (I mark them on the top tape border of the design beforehand.) In

pencil draw an outline of the correct dimensions on the brown paper. *Make sure corners are square.*

4. Dampen the wrong side of the canvas with a sponge dipped in cold water, or sprinkle the canvas with cold water until it is damp all over. Or use a steam iron to steam-block it.

5. Lay the canvas face down on the brown paper. See how it conforms to the outline. Pull or stretch the canvas to conform to the outline. Tack it down at ½-inch to 1-inch intervals as needed. Work with an even tension. Work from the centers of each side out. After you put a tack in one side, go to the diagonally opposite side and pull and tack.

6. Leave until dry—about 48 hours.

Mounting a Pillow

1. Place blocked canvas right side in—face to face with right side of backing of your choice.

2. Allow a seam allowance of 3 or more stitched rows all around; pin or baste into place.

3. Hand-sew or machine-stitch (use heavy-duty attachment or machine, if necessary) on three sides.

4. Trim excess canvas ⅝ inch from stitching line.

5. Trim excess backing ⅝ inch from stitching line.

6. Clip corners for turning.

7. Reverse pillow. Fill through opening with dacron, foam rubber, or pillow form.

8. Sew opening together by hand.

Mounting a Wall Hanging

Method A:
Have the art store mount the piece on canvas stretchers. If you wish to do this yourself, and do not know how to mount canvas on canvas stretchers, your art store will undoubtedly show you how, telling you what tools you need to use: either hammer and tacks or a staple gun and staples. Once the wall hanging is mounted on canvas stretchers, it can be framed or hung as is.

Method B:
1. Mount the blocked canvas on ¼-inch plywood, allowing a foldover of at least 4 stitched rows all around.

2. Attach to plywood with small upholstery tacks, stretching as you apply. Tack on the back, not on the front.

3. The back of the hanging can be covered with a piece of felt, using tacks or glue.

4. The wall hanging can be framed or hung as it is.

More detailed information about blocking and mounting needlepoint pieces can be found in:

Needlepoint for Everyone, by Mary Brooks Picken and Doris White with Claire Valentine. New York: Harper & Row, Publishers, 1970.

Needlepoint, by Hope Hanley. New York: Charles Scribner's Sons, 1964.

Directory of Needlework Shops

Most department stores have needlework departments. Visit your favorite store in your home town or a nearby town. The author has visited only those stores marked by asterisks. This list has been compiled from published sources currently available. It is advisable to check local telephone and other directories for possible address changes.

Store names are listed in alphabetical order by city and within state.

Arizona

Busy Work
P.O. Box 1389
Phoenix, Arizona 85001

Camelback Knitting Shop
4812 North 7th Avenue
Phoenix, Arizona 85013

The Yarn Tree
7051 Fifth Avenue, Suite "L"
Scottsdale, Arizona 85251

Yarn Carousel
18 North Tucson Boulevard
Tucson, Arizona 85016

California

The Nimble Thimble
MAILING ADDRESS:
P.O. Box 713
Aptos, California 95003

STUDIO ADDRESS:
119 Alta Drive
La Selva, California 95076

Haystack Ltd. Inc.
240 South Beverly Drive
Beverly Hills, California 90212

Port O'Call
11965 San Vincente
Brentwood, California 94513

Yarn Barn
16561 Ventura Boulevard
Encino, California 91316

Loretto Needlepoint Studio
150 South Fairfax Avenue
(Farmer's Market)
Los Angeles, California 90036

Petit Point Junction
373 North Robertson Boulevard
Los Angeles, California 90048

Tina of California
1156 North McCadden Place
Los Angeles, California 90038

Laisy Daisy Needlecraft Shop, Inc.
602 East Walnut Street
Pasadena, California 91101

Nimble Needle
2645 San Diego Avenue
San Diego, California 92110

Determined Productions, Inc.
Box 2150
San Francisco, California 94126

The Knittery
2040 Union Street
San Francisco, California 94123

The Yarn Depot, Inc.
545 Sutter Street
San Francisco, California 94102

Mrs. Loretto B. Link
1228 State Street
Santa Barbara, California 93104

Handcraft from Europe Importers
P.O. Box 372
Sausalito, California 94965

The Needlecraft Shop, Inc.
4501 Van Nuys Blvd.
Sherman Oaks, California 91403

Colorado

The Wild Plum
517 Wilcox Street
P.O. Box 512
Castle Rock, Colorado 80104

Connecticut

Valley Handcrafters
Sub. of Wm. E. Wright Co.
152 Simsbury Road
Avon, Connecticut 06001

Entre Nous
1089 Post Road
Darien, Connecticut 06820

The Handcraft Shoppe
Goodwives Shopping Plaza
Darien, Connecticut 06820

Needleloft Inc.
Mill Lane
Farmington, Connecticut 06032

The Designing Woman, Inc.
Lakeville, Connecticut 06039

Knitters World, Inc.
394 Middle Turnpike West
Manchester, Connecticut 06040

Mili Holmes' Studio
95 Colonial Road
New Canaan, Connecticut 06840

Ellly
P.O. Box 3898
New Haven, Connecticut 06525

Yarncraft Inc.
242 Sound Beach Avenue
Old Greenwich, Connecticut 06970

The Yarnbee
413 Main Street
Ridgefield, Connecticut 06877

Village Needlework Shop
293 Pequot Road
Southport, Connecticut 06490

Freeman's Pickwick Yarns
Main Street
Stamford, Connecticut 06901

Hook 'N' Needle
Old Sasco Mill
1869 East State Street
Westport, Connecticut 06880

Washington, D.C.

American Needlework Center, Inc.
2803 M Street, N.W.
Washington, D.C. 20007

The Elegant Needle, Ltd.
5430 MacArthur Boulevard N.W.
Washington, D.C. 20016

Greengage
P.O. Box 9683
Washington,D.C. 20016

The Woolgatherer
1608 20th Street, N.W.
Washington, D.C. 20009

Delaware

Country House of Yarn
R.D. #1
P.O. Box 268
Dover, Delaware 19901

Colonial Yarn Shop
3830 Kennet Pike
Wilmington, Delaware 19807

Florida

The Flying Needles
2935 West Bay Drive
Belleair Bluffs, Florida 33540

Yarn and Design Studio
4061 Ponce de Leon Boulevard
Coral Gables, Florida 33146

Yarns Galore
2422 Ponce de Leon
Coral Gables, Florida 33134

Bishop Woodside Yarns
633 North Grandview Avenue
Daytona Beach, Florida 32018

Helen Hill
518 East Atlantic Boulevard
Delray Beach, Florida 33444

Yarns Galore
2306 East Oakland Park Boulevard
(S.E. corner U.S. 1)
Fort Lauderdale, Florida 33306

Needlecrafts
2941 Corinthian Avenue
Jacksonville, Florida 32210.

Knit & Needle
212 East Orange
Lakeland, Florida 33801

Little River Knit Shop
8212 North East 2nd Avenue
Miami, Florida 33138

Lucy Cooper Hill
1126 Kane Concourse
Bay Harbor Islands
Miami Beach, Florida 33154

Love and Stitches
P.O. Box 3051, Ocean View
Miami Beach, Florida 33140

Yarns Galore
1230 N.E. 163rd Street
N. Miami Beach, Florida 33162

Needlepoint Design
312 Worth Avenue
Palm Beach, Florida 33480

Smith Knudsen Inc.
Worth Avenue
Palm Beach, Florida 33480

Spinning Wheel Yarn Shop
1816 South Osprey
Sarasota, Florida 33579

Needlecraft Studio
4241 El Prado Boulevard
Tampa, Florida 33609

Ruthelmas Yarn Basket
500 Orchid Springs Drive
Winter Haven, Florida 33880

Georgia

Papillon
Cates Plaza
375 Pharr Road, N.E.
Atlanta, Georgia 30305

The Snail's Pace, Inc.
548 East Paces Ferry Road, N.E.
Atlanta, Georgia 30305

The Yardstick
Medical Arts Shopping Center
4841 Waters Avenue
Savannah, Georgia 31404

Illinois

Needle Mania
(on second floor of Couture, Ltd.)
66 East Walton Place
Chicago, Illinois 60611

Ball O Yarn
146 Merchant Street
Decatur, Illinois 62523

LeeWards
P.O. Box 903
1200 St. Charles Street
Elgin, Illinois 60120

Knit One Purl Too
657 Vernon Avenue
Glencoe, Illinois 60022

Lake Forest Sports Shop
265 Market Square
Lake Forest, Illinois 60045

Sanpie
"The Needle Arts"
179 East Deerpath Avenue
Lake Forest, Illinois 60045

Knit and Purl
Belvidere Mall
Waukegan, Illinois 60085

The Needleperson
Willowbrook Plaza
6942 Kingery Highway
Willowbrook, Illinois

Indiana

Ziesel's Downtown
Elkhart, Indiana 46514

Schoolhouse Too
100 Center Complex
Mishawaka, Indiana 46544

Iowa

The Hobbycraft Shop
801–803 Jefferson
Burlington, Iowa 52601

Kansas

In Stitches
3901 Prairie Lane
Prairie Village, Kansas 66208

The Enchanted Cottage
3107 East Central
Wichita, Kansas 67214

Kentucky

Maud Hundley Studio, Inc.
12204 U.S. Highway 60
Middletown, Kentucky 40243

MAILING ADDRESS:
Box 264
Anchorage, Kentucky 40223

Louisiana

Angel's Needlecraft Shop
602 East Morris Avenue
Hammond, Louisiana 70401

Elbers Knitting Shop
837 Short Street
New Orleans, Louisiana 70118

Needlepoint, Inc.
2401 Magazine Street
New Orleans, Louisiana 70130

The Quarter Stitch
532 St. Peter Street
   on Jackson Square
New Orleans, Louisiana 70130

The Lusianne
127 Kings Highway
Shreveport, Louisiana 71104

Maine

Needle Arts, Inc.
28 Washington Street
Camden, Maine 04843

Maryland

Baltimore Needlepoint Shop
2510 North Charles Street
Baltimore, Maryland 21218

Desiree Design Studio for Needlecrafts
7942 Wisconsin Avenue
Suite 122–24
Bethesda, Maryland

Massachusetts

Nimble Fingers Inc.
283 Dartmouth Street
Boston, Massachusetts 02116

The Golden Eye
Box 205
Chestnut Hill, Massachusetts 02167

Country Needle
Cushing Plaza
Route 3
Cohasset, Massachusetts 02025

Skein & Spool Shop
714 Bliss Road
Longmeadow, Massachusetts 01106

The Crafts Centre
Quaker Road
Nantucket, Massachusetts 02554

Nantucket Needleworks
11 South Water Street
Nantucket, Massachusetts 02554

The Stitchery
RETAIL SHOP:
68 Central Street
Wellesley Hills, Massachusetts 02181

MAIL ORDER:
204 Worcester Street
Wellesley Hills, Massachusetts 02181

Elsa Williams, Inc.
Needlecraft House
West Townsend, Massachusetts 01474

Margot Hamilton Needlepoint
4 River Road
Worthington, Massachusetts 01098

Michigan

Berkley Knit Shop
2688 Coolidge Highway
Berkley, Michigan 48072

Needlepoint A La Carte
325 South Woodward
Birmingham, Michigan 48011

Yarncraft
Birmingham, Michigan 48011

The Little Red Schoolhouse
P.O. Box 148
Dowagiac, Michigan 49047

Peacock Alley
650 Crosswell Street, S.E.
Grand Rapids, Michigan 49506

Yarncraft
341 Fisher Road
Grosse Pointe, Michigan 48236

Polachek Fabric
109 West Michigan Street
Jackson, Michigan 49201

Fenstemacher's Fabric and Yarn Shop
305 South Washington Street
Lansing, Michigan 48933

The Sampler
1011 S. Washington
Royal Oak, Michigan 48067

Minnesota

The Jeweled Needle
1009 Nicollet Mall
Minneapolis, Minnesota 55402

Stitch Niche, Inc.
2866 Hennepin Avenue, South
Minneapolis, Minnesota 55408

Mississippi

Celita's
Old Canton Road Plaza
Jackson, Mississippi 39216

Pandora's Box
P.O. Box E
Merigold, Mississippi 38759

Missouri

The Studio
316 West 63rd Street
Kansas City, Missouri 64113

The Krick Kit Co.
31 North Brentwood Boulevard
St. Louis, Missouri 63105

Montana

Shoppers Bazaar
Central Avenue
Great Falls, Montana 59401

Nebraska

The Needlepoint Studio
8707 Shamrock Road
Omaha, Nebraska 68114

New Jersey

Astor Place Ltd.
111 Morristown Road
Bernardsville, New Jersey 07924

American Crewel and Canvas Studio
P.O. Box 298
Boonton, New Jersey 07005

Crafty Women
Colts Town Shoppes
Highway 34
Colts Neck, New Jersey 07722

Stitch Witchery
Denbrook Village
Route 10
Denville, New Jersey 07834

Mona Spoor Associates
22 Beverly Place
Edgewater, New Jersey 07020

Threadneedle
7 East Palisade
Englewood, New Jersey 07631

Dee Needlepoint Originals
P.O. Box 1756
Point Pleasant, New Jersey 08742

Nassau's Inc.
235 East Ridgewood Avenue
Ridgewood, New Jersey 07450

Janet's
Highway 35
Sea Girt, New Jersey 08750

Nan M. Samons
589 Valley Road
West Orange, New Jersey 07052

New Mexico

Greer's Knit and Reweave
1711 San Pedro, N.E.
Albuquerque, New Mexico 87110

New York

The Knitting Needle*
144 Bedford Road
Armonk, New York 10504

T. E. Doegler
Box 126
Blauvelt, New York 10913

Goldman's Yarn Stores, Inc.
2540 Grand Concourse
Bronx, New York 10458

Goldman's Yarn Stores, Inc.
301 E. Kingsbridge Road
Bronx, New York 10458

Bell Yarn Co., Inc.
10 Box Street
Brooklyn, New York 11222

Goldman's Yarn Stores, Inc.
4417 13th Avenue
Brooklyn, New York 11219

Silver Needle, Inc.
29 King Street
Chappaqua, New York 10514

Four Wives, Inc.
43 Main Street
Cold Spring Harbor, New York 11724

The Needle Nook*
at the Village Clock
Copake, New York 12516

Hilde's Knit Shop
305 White Plains Road
Eastchester, New York 10707

The Point
26 Glenwood Road
Glen Head, New York 11545

The Open Door to Stitchery
4 Bond Street
Great Neck, New York 11021

Studio One
Halstead Avenue and Osborne Road
Harrison, New York 10926

Needlecraft
136 Chatsworth Avenue
Larchmont, New York 10538

Joan Pryor
1965-B Palmer Avenue
Larchmont, New York 10538

Fabric and Notion Shop
1335 Halstead Avenue
Mamaroneck, New York 10543

Katherine Knox
445 Plandome Road
Manhasset, New York 11030

Millbrook Needlework Guild
Millbrook, New York 12545

B. Altman & Co.
Art Needlework Department
Fifth Avenue and 34th Street
New York, New York 10016

Bloomingdale's
Needlepoint and Yarn Department
Lexington Avenue and 59th Street
New York, New York 10022

Boutique Margot*
26 West 54 Street
New York, New York 10019

Coulter Studios, Inc.*
118 East 59 Street
New York, New York 10022

Suzy Girard
1042 Lexington Avenue
New York, New York 10021

In-Stitches
356 East 19 Street
New York, New York 10003

The Ladies Hobby Shop
780 Madison Avenue
New York, New York 10021

The Ladies Hobby Shop
2350 Broadway
New York, New York 10024

Macy's
Herald Square
New York, New York 10001

Alice Maynard*
724 Fifth Avenue
New York, New York 10022

Mazaltov's Inc.*
758 Madison Avenue
New York, New York 10020

B. J. Mitchell
14 East 6 Street
New York, New York 10022

Museum Recreations, Inc.
220 East 57 Street
Suite 2B
New York, New York 10022

Nina Needlepoint
860 Madison Avenue
New York, New York 10021

Needle Point Boutique
Lord and Taylor
Fifth Avenue at 38 Street
New York, New York 10018

Needlepoint Design by Lou Gartner*
Bergdorf Goodman
754 Fifth Avenue
New York, New York 10019

The Needle Points
979 Third Avenue
New York, New York 10022

Selma's Art Needlework*
1645 Second Avenue
New York, New York 10028

Sue's Needlepoint*
1235 First Avenue
New York, New York 10021

Titillations, Ltd.
211 East 60 Street
New York, New York 10022

Two Needles
1283 Madison Avenue
New York, New York 10028

Erica Wilson*
717 Madison Avenue
New York, New York 10021

The Wool Farm
49 East 10 Street
New York, New York 10003

The Wool Gallery
141 East 62 Street
New York, New York 10021

Woolworks, Inc.*
783 Madison Avenue
New York, New York 10021

Black Sheep
48 Purchase Street
Rye, New York 10580

Handy Lady
72 Garth Road
Scarsdale, New York 10583

Wild & Wooly
18 New Dorp Lane
Staten Island, New York 10306

The Knit Nook
324 South Salina Street
Syracuse, New York 13202

Hobby Yarns
217 Main Street
White Plains, New York 10601

Morris Yarn Co.
188 Martine Avenue
White Plains, New York 10601

Needlepoint Design by Lou Gartner
Bergdorf Goodman
Maple Avenue
White Plains, New York 10601

The Needleworks*
90 East Post Road
White Plains, New York 10601

North Carolina

Ruth Leary
382 North Elm Street
Greensboro, North Carolina 27401

Ohio

Madge Erf Needlework
45 East Washington Street
Chagrin Falls, Ohio 44022

Madge Erf
16819 Chagrin Boulevard
Cleveland, Ohio 44120

Kaleidoscope Needlework
2525 North Reynolds Road
Toledo, Ohio 43615

Arlene's Yarn Ship
5552 Secor Road
Toledo, Ohio 43623

Oklahoma

Josie-Carter, Inc.
2422 North Robinson
Oklahoma City, Oklahoma 73103

The Yarn Garden, Inc.
10956 North May Avenue
(in Quail Plaza)
Oklahoma City, Oklahoma 73120

Handcraft Shop
1405 East 15 Street
Tulsa, Oklahoma 74120

Miljan Studios
1830 Utica Square
Tulsa, Oklahoma 74144

Pennsylvania

Le Petit Point Boutique
17 East Lancaster Avenue
Ardmore, Pennsylvania 19003

The Needlework Studio, Inc.
Bryn Mawr and Summit Grove Avenues
Bryn Mawr, Pennsylvania 19010

The Needlecrafters*
64 South Pitt Street
Carlisle, Pennsylvania 17013

Needlepoint Corner
8121 Old York Road
Elkins Park, Pennsylvania 19117

Creative Stitchery
2116 Walnut Street
Philadelphia, Pennsylvania 19103

The Needle's Eye
1724 Sansom Street
Philadelphia, Pennsylvania 19103

Sawyer Needlepoint
8611 Germantown Avenue
Philadelphia, Pennsylvania 19118

Sophisti-Kits
P.O. Box 5020
Pittsburgh, Pennsylvania 15206

The Sinkler Studio
223 Iven Avenue
Box 93
Radnor, Pennsylvania 19087

Rhode Island

Betty Schloss Handicraft Studio
187 Westminister Mall
Providence, Rhode Island 02903

South Carolina

Porter's Gift Shop
Florence Mall
P.O. Box 3037
Florence, South Carolina 29501

Tennessee

The Yarn Barn
1301 Madison Avenue
Memphis, Tennessee 38104

Nancy McCauley's Canvas Patch Originals
P.O. Box 3072
Oak Ridge, Tennessee 37830

Texas

The Establishment
Deux Amis, Inc.
3708 Crawford
Austin, Texas 78731

Clever Needlewoman, Inc.
25A Highland Park Village
Dallas, Texas 75205

Knit-Wit Shop
6021 North Berkshire Lane
Dallas, Texas 75225

Needlework Patio
6925 Snider Plaza
Dallas, Texas 75205

Gaye Weyand Needlecraft
358 Park Forest Center
Dallas, Texas 75229

Circle Knit Shop
3465 Bluebonnet Circle
Fort Worth, Texas 76109

Merribee Needle Art Co.
2904 West Lancaster Street
Fort Worth, Texas 76107

The Silver Needle Hobby Shop
6100 Camp Bowie Boulevard
Fort Worth, Texas 76116

Burrow Knit Shop
2150 Portsmouth
Houston, Texas 77006

Chaparral
2505 River Oaks Boulevard
Houston, Texas 77019

The Knit Shop
3516 South Shepherd at Richmond
Houston, Texas 77006

Virginia Maxwell
Custom Needlework Studio
3404 Kirby Drive
Houston, Texas 77006

Needle Nuts
5207 Kelvin
Houston, Texas 77005

Vernon Harris Knit Shop
1310 Avenue "Q"
Lubbock, Texas 79401

Virginia

Yarns Etcetera
215 King Street
Alexandria, Virginia 22314

The Needlework Shop
Baaracks Road Shopping Center
Charlottesville, Virginia 22203

The Knitting Shop
140 South Catoctin Circle
Leesburg, Virginia 22075

Knit N Needle Shop
7552A Waros Corner
Shopping Center
Norfolk, Virginia

Laura Weaver Needlework
Hotel Patrick Henry
617 South Jefferson Street
Roanoke, Virginia 24011

Washington

World of Fabrics
Olympia, Washington 98501

The Yarn Barn, Inc.
Route 4, Box 660
Poulsbo, Washington 98370

Phalice's Thread Web
West 1301 14th Avenue
Spokane, Washington 99204

Wisconsin

Ruhama's Yarns & Fabrics
420 East Silver Spring Drive
Milwaukee, Wisconsin 53217

Frederick Herrshner, Co.
Hoover Road
Stevens Point, Wisconsin 54481

Wyoming

Georgette's
2304 Pioneer Street
Cheyenne, Wyoming 82001

Bucky King
King Bros. Ranch
Box 124C
Buffalo Star Route
Sheridan, Wyoming 82801

Bibliography

ALBERS, ANNI. *On Weaving*. Middletown, Conn.: Wesleyan University Press, 1965.

ALBERS, JOSEF. *Interaction of Color*. New Haven, Conn.: Yale University Press, 1971.

ANDERSON, DONALD M. *Elements of Design*. New York: Holt, Rinehart & Winston, 1961.

BATES, KENNETH F. *Basic Design, Principles and Practice*. New York: The World Publishing Company, 1964.

BERENSON, BERNARD. *The Italian Painters of the Renaissance*. Volume II, The Florentine Painters, the Central Italian Painters. London: Phaidon, 1968.

BUCHER, JO. *Complete Guide to Creative Needlepoint*. Des Moines, Iowa: Creative Home Library, 1973.

————. *The Complete Guide to Embroidery Stitches and Crewel*. Des Moines, Iowa: Creative Home Library, 1971.

DENDEL, ESTHER WARNER. *Needleweaving, Easy as Embroidery*. Philadelphia: Countryside Press, 1971.

DONNELLY, BARBARA H., and GULLERS, KARL W. *The Crewel Needlepoint World*, New York, Stockholm and Copenhagen: Gullers International, Inc., 1973.

ENTHOVEN, JACQUELINE. *Stitchery for Children: A Manual for Teachers, Parents, and Children*. New York: Van Nostrand Reinhold Company, 1968.

GARTNER, LOUIS J., JR. *Needlepoint Design*. New York: William Morrow & Company, 1970.

GOMBRICH, E. H. *Art and Illusion, A Study in the Psychology of Pictorial Representation*. Princeton, N.J.: Princeton University Press, 1960.

GRAHAM, DONALD W. *Composing Pictures*. New York: Van Nostrand Reinhold Company, 1970.

HANLEY, HOPE. *Needlepoint*. New York: Charles Scribner's Sons, 1964.

————. *Needlepoint in America*. New York: Charles Scribner's Sons, 1969.

HICKS, DAVID. *David Hicks on Decoration—with fabrics*. New York: World Publishing, 1971.

HOLSTEIN, JONATHAN. *Abstract Design in American Quilts*. New York: Whitney Museum of Art, 1971.

IREYS, KATHARINE. *The Encyclopedia of Canvas Embroidery Stitch Patterns*. New York: Thomas Y. Crowell Company, 1972.

ITTEN, JOHANNES. *Design and Form, The Basic Course at the Bauhaus*. New York: Van Nostrand Reinhold, 1964.

————. *The Art of Color: The Subjective Experience and Objective Rationale of Color*. New York: Reinhold Publishing Corporation, 1961.

JACOBSON, EGBERT. *Basic Color, An Interpretation of the Ostwald Color System*. Chicago: Paul Theobald, 1948.

JOHN, EDITH. *Filling Stitches*. Newton Center, Mass.: Charles T. Branford Company, 1967.

JUSTEMA, WILLIAM and DORIS. *Weaving and Needlecraft Color Course*. New York: Van Nostrand Reinhold Company, 1971.

KARASZ, MARISKA. *Adventures in Stitches*. New York: Funk & Wagnalls Company, 1949.

KELDER, DIANE (Ed.). *Stuart Davis*. New York: Praeger Publishers, 1971.

KLEE, PAUL. *Paul Klee on Modern Art*. London: Faber and Faber, Ltd., MCML.

LURCAT, JEAN. *Designing Tapestry*. London: Rockliff, 1950.

McCall's Decorating Book, by the Decorating Editors of McCall's. New York: Random House–McCall's, 1964.

100 Embroidery Stitches. Anchor Embroidery Stitches. New York: Charles Scribner's Sons, 1967.

PETERSON, GRETE, and SVENNAS, ELSIE. *Handbook of Stitches*. New York: Van Nostrand Reinhold Company, 1970.

PICKEN, MARY BROOKS, and WHITE, DORIS, with VALENTINE, CLAIRE. *Needlepoint for Everyone*. New York: Harper & Row, Publishers, 1970.

RAINEY, SARITA R. *Weaving Without a Loom*. New York: Davis Publications, Inc., 1971.

REILLY, ESTHER HUNTINGTON. *At Home with Decorating*. Radnor, Pa.: Chilton Book Company, 1971.

RILEY, NORMAN (Ed.). *Butterflies and Moths.* Text by Alfred Werner and Josef Bijok. Revised Edition. New York: The Viking Press, 1970.

SIDNEY, SYLVIA, with LEWIS, ALFRED ALLAN. *Sylvia Sidney Needlepoint Book.* New York: Van Nostrand Reinhold Company, 1968.

SLOAN, PATRICIA. *Color: Basic Principles and New Directions.* London: Studio Vista, 1968.

SPRINGALL, DIANA. *Canvas Embroidery.* Newton Center, Mass.: Charles T. Branford Company, 1969 and B. T. Batsford Limited, London.

SUTHERLAND, GRAHAM. *The Coventry Tapestry.* London: The Pallas Gallery, 1964.

WILSON, ERICA. *Erica Wilson's Embroidery Book.* New York: Charles Scribner's Sons, 1973.

Notes

1. Barbara H. Donnelly and Karl W. Gullers, *The Crewel Needlepoint World.* Gullers International, Inc. New York, Stockholm and Copenhagen: 1973. P. 35.

"SCOOP: A term meaning that once you have come to the front of the canvas from the back with your yarn to start your stitchery, you bend the canvas so the needle goes through the front to the back and comes out in front with the point all in one motion, and pulls through on the front keeping your right hand on front of the canvas."

2. Donald W. Graham, *Composing Pictures.* New York: Van Nostrand Reinhold Company, 1970. P. 105.

"One of the most successful design contrasts is that of a sharp, crisp, or hard element played against a soft element."

3. Katharine Ireys, *The Encyclopedia of Canvas Embroidery Stitch Patterns.* New York: Thomas Y. Crowell Company, 1972. P. 99.

This stitch is shown and called Diagonal Satin over three threads and four threads. It is also shown in Donnelly and Gullers, *op. cit.,* on page 46.

4. *Stuart Davis,* edited by Diane Kelder. New York: Praeger Publishers, 1971. Pp. 34, 35.

"In the areas of the work for example there must be a unit of area that dominates all the areas, so that one looking at the picture will instinctively feel a simple order between them. He will feel that this area is half of that one and that this one is twice that. In color the same thing holds, namely, there is a dominant color to which all the other colors bear a simple numerical relation to one another. When I say *simple* I mean that the work must be right in the way I have mentioned and that if the artist combines only a few simple elements correctly he will have created beauty; needless to say if any one is clever enough to carry this order unerringly into the most subtle and complicated relations he is that much more profound. In the illusionary element of *relief* again the law holds good. If a given plane has a suggested relief of half an inch then all other planes in the picture must have a simple mathematical relation to that one which we will assume is the dominant plane. In textures, suggested or actual, the same rule holds. In the element of *line* there must be a simple relation of continuity which in one sense is its area. Then there is the factor of *third dimensional balance* that must be taken into consideration. This has to do with the suggested weights of the various planes of the picture. Their weights must be so arranged that if the planes were actual and the picture were placed in a horizontal position they would be in perfect balance like a building. Of all these elements that go to make the painting there is naturally one that will dominate the others. In different pictures different elements will dominate. In most cases the dominant element is strong enough to dominate and make seem orderly lack of order in the other elements, just as in a jazz band the powerful rhythm holds together the most unrelated excursions of the individual pieces. In a word a work of art can only exist as a consistent unit with its own logic."

5. I found a butterfly specimen with similar colors in *Butterflies and Moths,* Norman Riley, Editor, Text by Alfred Werner and Josef Bijok (New York: The Viking Press, 1970) P. 100, Plate 23: *Sasakia Charonda*).

6. Mary Brooks Picken and Doris White with Claire

Valentine, *Needlepoint for Everyone*. New York: Harper & Row, Publishers, 1970. P. 87.

"*Sizing or Stiffening*. Panels, rugs, and pieces that are not mounted, as well as handbags, luggage and items which will be handled, should be sized in order for them to keep their shape.

"Before removing tacks after blocking and drying, apply a very thin coating of sizing to the back of the worked area.

"Dry glue can be purchased from hardware and artist supply stores. Mix according to directions on the package, making only enough for immediate use as this type of glue will not keep. Spread with a knife or with a stiff brush. Cover completely but do not work glue into the surface. Remove any excess and let dry."

7. Jo Bucher, *The Complete Guide to Embroidery Stitches and Crewel*. Des Moines, Iowa: Creative Home Library, 1971. P. 293.

8. Mary Brooks Picken and Doris White with Claire Valentine, *op. cit.*, p. 72.

"Tramé is an UNDERLAY of colored yarn thread placed over the horizontal meshes that are close together in double-thread canvas. The purpose of tramé is to indicate the design and change of colors on the canvas. In this case yarn is used instead of painting the canvas."

9. Jo Bucher, *Complete Guide to Creative Needlepoint*. Des Moines, Iowa: Creative Home Library, 1973. P. 225.

10. Sylvia Sidney with Alfred Allan Lewis, *Sylvia Sidney Needlepoint Book*. New York: Van Nostrand Reinhold Company, 1968. P. 49.

"Tramé is a series of long stitches executed in either silk or split wool done on the canvas as a backing; the regular stitches are worked over it. It functions in roughly the same way for needlepoint as underpainting for an oil painting. It gives the work greater body and so is especially valuable when you are using the Half-Cross Stitch. It is also very useful in multicolored or toned pieces—you use the same colors that you will use in the regular stitching, so you can get a clear idea of how they will harmonize. Tramé is easy to do and well worth the little extra time it takes."

11. There are interesting discussions and examples of Laid Work fillings in:

Jo Bucher, *The Complete Guide to Embroidery Stitches and Crewel*. Pp. 248–53.

Edith John, *Filling Stitches*. Newton Center, Mass.: Charles T. Branford Company, 1967. Pp. 13–36: Couched Fillings; pp. 37–57: Lacy and Miscellaneous.

12. Jo Bucher, *The Complete Guide to Embroidery Stitches and Crewel*. P. 42.

The Recent Burden Stitch is defined as ". . . a combination of Laid Work and Brick Stitch. This stitch can be used very nicely in shading, and the spacing of both overstitching and Laid Work can give you some unique effects. By using a different color of thread for Laid Work than for the surface stitchery and working the stitches close together, you can obtain an effect of weaving. You can add an interesting texture by spacing out your top stitching and having the background part of the overall effect."

13. Walter A. Wittich and Charles F. Schuller, *Instructional Technology: Its Nature and Use*. Fifth edition. New York: Harper & Row, 1973.

14. The seven color contrasts that I discuss are described by Johannes Itten in *Design and Form, The Basic Course at the Bauhaus* and *The Art of Color* (New York: Reinhold Publishing Corporation, 1961) under the following names: Hue, Light-Dark, Cold-Warm, Complementary, Simultaneous, Saturation, Extension.

15. *Paul Klee on Modern Art*. London: Faber and Faber, Ltd., MCML. P. 23.

"Colour is primarily Quality. Secondly, it is also Weight, for it has not only colour value but brilliance. Thirdly, it is Measure, for besides Quality and Weight, it has its limits, its area and its extent, all of which may be measured."

16. Egbert Jacobson, *Basic Color, An Interpretation of the Ostwald Color System*. Chicago: Paul Theobald, 1948.

A similar idea is expressed on page 28:
"The circle shows how colors vary in hue.
A yellow may be made redder or greener.
A red may be made yellower or bluer.
A blue may be made redder or greener.
A green may be made bluer or yellower."

17. Egbert Jacobson, *ibid*. Pp. 22–25.

18. Johannes Itten, *Design and Form, The Basic Course at the Bauhaus*. P. 42.

"The greatest contrast effect is reached with the colors orange-red and blue-green. All other colors appear cold or warm according to their juxtaposition with warmer or colder values."

19. *Paul Klee on Modern Art*. See Note 15.

20. *Stuart Davis*. See Note 4.

21. Johannes Itten, *Design and Form, The Basic Course at the Bauhaus*. P. 43.

"The simultaneous contrast:

Its effect is based on a corresponding law of complementaries. Each pure color physiologically demands its opposite color or complementary. If it is not present, the eye simultaneously produces the complementary color. A strong green makes an adjoining neutral appear reddish gray; a strong red gives a greenish effect to the same gray."

22. Sarita R. Rainey, *Weaving Without a Loom*. New York: Davis Publications, Inc., 1971. P. 11.

"Color inspires, motivates, accents, sets mood, evokes atmosphere."

23. *Paul Klee on Modern Art*. See Note 15.

24. Mary Brooks Picken and Doris White with Claire Valentine, *op. cit.*, p. 51.

"Value refers to the lightness or darkness of a color. The lighter the color, the higher is its value. The term ' value' has nothing to do with the intensity of a color, but refers solely to the gradations between the extremes of light and dark."

25. Josef Albers, *Interaction of Color*. New Haven, Conn.: Yale University Press, 1971. Pp. 12–13.

"However, it is still true that only a minority can distinguish the lighter from the darker within close intervals when obscured by contrasting hues or by different color intensities.

"In order to correct a prejudice common among painters and designers—that they belong to that minority —we have the students test themselves. We confront them with several pairs of color, from which they are to select and to record which color in a pair is the darker. The darker one, it is explained, is visually the heavier one, or the one containing more black, or less white. It should be mentioned that the students are encouraged to abstain from making a judgment in any case of doubt. It may also demonstrate that not voting can have a positive meaning.

"Though there have always been advanced painting students in the basic color class, the result of this test has remained constant for a number of years: 60% of the answers are wrong and only 40% are right, not counting the undecided cases."

26. Jean Lurcat, *Designing Tapestry*. London: Rockliff, 1950. A similar approach is described on pages 39–41.

27. E. H. Gombrich, *Art and Illusion, A Study in the Psychology of Pictorial Representation*. Princeton, N.J.: Princeton University Press, 1960. Pp. 43–44.

". . . one of the earliest examples of the chiaroscuro woodcut technique. By lowering the tone of the ground the artist can now use the white of the paper to indicate light. The gain from this modest extension of range is dramatic, for these indications of light not only increase the sense of modeling but also convey to us what we call 'texture'—the way, that is, in which light behaves when it strikes a particular surface. It is only in the chiaroscuro version of the woodcut, therefore, that we get the 'feel' of the scaly body of the serpent."

28. *David Hicks on Decoration—with fabrics*. New York: World Publishing, 1971. Introduction.

"But if you want to mix patterns a simple rule is to look for the greatest possible variety in scale and for a connecting link between several different patterns which can be one or more colours or a similar motif or characteristic."

29. *Ibid*.

"Textural interest in the fabric can add greatly to charm and interest of furniture placed in immediate proximity."

30. Esther Huntington Reilly, *At Home with Decorating*. Radnor, Pa.: Chilton Book Company, 1971. Pp. 68–69.

"My favorite reading spot is a corner arrangement having two comfortable chairs face and share the same ottoman or footstool and a large table holding a good reading lamp to fill the corner in between them. It makes an ideal spot for husband and wife togetherness, if the children haven't grabbed it first. The table can be square or round with a skirt added for color. If the husband is a bug on being surrounded by tons of reading material, the table can be quite large, thirty by fifty-four inches, with a shelf below. It becomes a great spot with a reading chair and ottoman placed on the long side and my lady's smaller lounge on the short side. This can be an excellent arrangement when the wall is somewhat long and there is extra space to be filled."

31. A good explanation of photostating is found in *Needlepoint Design*, by Louis J. Gartner, Jr. (New York: William Morrow & Company, Inc., 1970), on pages 56, 61, 184 and 185:

"You can change the size of any design or motif by taking it to a shop that does photostatic enlargements. You may want to blow up a picture or a section of a picture in order then to trace the larger version. Or you may already have made a tracing, from a book or section of wallpaper or fabric, which you want enlarged. (Make the tracing in ink with a fine-line marker.) For that matter, you can have things reduced in size, too, if you want. In any case, the change in size has to be made before you transfer the design to canvas. . . . Costs of photostats differ all over the country, but it is safe to say that a photostat is cheaper than having a photographic print made of your subject. It is intended to be temporary and is therefore made on inexpensive paper and it will eventually fade. All you have to tell the shop is the overall size of the picture or of the part of the picture you need; tell them to blow it up to six inches or ten inches or whatever you want. Ask for a positive print.

"Some photostat shops may not have the facilities for printing a very large stat such as a rug design all in one piece. You can persuade them to blow the design up in sections, all to the same scale, and then tape them together.

"Depending on where you live, you may or may not have easy access to photostating shops, or may have trouble getting very large stats for projects such as rugs. . . . If this is really a problem for you, the best thing to do is to look up, at the public library, in the Yellow Pages for the nearest large city in your area, the firms listed under 'Photo Copying.' Inquire by letter whether orders can be filled by mail and at what rates, explaining also the size of your original and the size of the stat that you want. There are hundreds of thousands of photo-copying shops across the country and their operations vary widely; in a major city you should be able to find at least one that can accommodate you. Be sure to specify that you want a photostat, as the same shops may do other, unnecessarily expensive types of photo copying."

Index